To Fair Isle and Back

Yellow-breasted Bunting - the ultimate achievement

(Where to Watch Birds? – On Stronsay!)

WRITTEN & ILLUSTRATED BY
JOHN HOLLOWAY

First Published August 1995
Stronsay Bird Reserve
Mill Bay, Stronsay
Orkney

ISBN 0-9526298-0-1

CONTENTS

All illustrations and photographs by the author

Front cover: Gyrfalcon – a 'garden bird' for the author on both Stronsay & Fair Isle

FOREWORD

We all at sometime dream of getting away to a remote island, perhaps of even owning a few acres of beautiful coastline. Many of us too dream of setting up our own nature reserve and watching it develop. Very few of us achieve either.

But it can be done!

In 1977 John Holloway and his family moved from Kent to Orkney with just such an idea, although it was not until 1989 that their own dream was realised with the opening of the Stronsay Bird Reserve adjacent to the beautiful sandy beach of Mill Bay.

The house 'Castle' and Reserve drive. The weedy turning circle to the right has hosted Rustic, Little and Yellow-breasted Buntings

The reserve is now well known throughout the U.K. and has featured in all the top ornithological magazines as a result of the many rare and interesting species which have been found there.

Much of this book revolves around John's time on Stronsay and coupled with his beautiful artwork gives a unique insight into island life. Not only are there illustrations of all the rare bird species seen on the island (except Red-throated Pipit which was only seen in flight!) but many evocative paintings of the island itself, from the rugged cliff-scenery of Odiness Bay to the

4

The logo of the Stronsay Bird Reserve, Yellow-breasted Bunting.
The reserve's ultimate achievement – one was found feeding
in the ripening oats in September 1992

tranquillity of a summer sunset at Bomasty Bay. There are paintings too of some of the most interesting island features peculiar to Orkney; the Odiness Drying-kiln; the Old courtyard of Holland Farm and many more, often depicted with a particular bird 'in situ'.

Fair Isle – where John and his family spent six happy years running the island shop is also featured and in particular the rare birds, on what is Britain's most isolated inhabited island.

Great Grey Shrike.
Rare and interesting species may turn up in the most unlikely places

Many new and interesting ornithological points are raised and the book contains a wealth of information on birds and bird-watching in Orkney and Shetland.

The bird illustrations are generally half-way between field-sketches and those found in 'field-guides' in order to complement the island views contained within the text and to convey the amount of detail seen in 'the field'.

All bird photographs were taken from the Reserve's car and in general reflect that exciting 'first glimpse' of a bird as experienced in the northern isles.

This book is not just a personal account, it is more an illustration of what can be achieved with a few acres and a lot of enthusiasm.

If you have read John's previous book 'Fair Isle's Garden Birds' and thrill at the idea of finding rare birds on your own 'local patch', then this book is a must. If you are interested in finding out more about birds and life in the northern isles, then read on....

Roderick Thorne

MAP OF STRONSAY

Stronsay, one of the 'North Isles' of Orkney,
is situated approximately 40 miles NNE of John o' Groats,
with Fair Isle a further 40 miles away to the NE.

The island is approximately 6 miles from 'corner' to 'corner'
and has a coastline of roughly 45 miles.

Auskerry (part of Stronsay) is a small detached island
approximately 3 miles to the South of 'The Pow'.

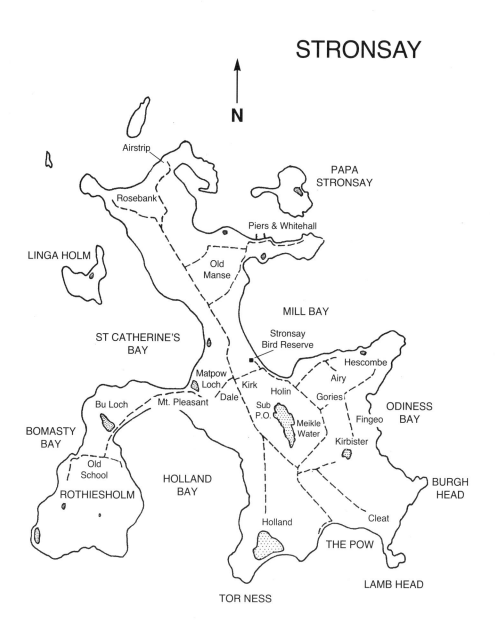

STRONSAY

N

Airstrip

Rosebank

PAPA STRONSAY

Piers & Whitehall

LINGA HOLM

Old Manse

MILL BAY

ST CATHERINE'S BAY

Stronsay Bird Reserve

Hescombe

Matpow Loch

Airy

Kirk

Holin

Gories

Bu Loch

Mt. Pleasant

Dale

Sub P.O.

Fingeo

ODINESS BAY

BOMASTY BAY

Meikle Water

Kirbister

Old School

ROTHIESHOLM

HOLLAND BAY

BURGH HEAD

Cleat

Holland

THE POW

LAMB HEAD

TOR NESS

"Every garden seemed to overflow with the most beautiful fuchsia hedges"

Chapter 1

STRONSAY - FIRST TIME AROUND

My wife Sue and I had done our homework very carefully, weighing-up the pro's and con's of all the Orkney Islands. Stronsay fitted the bill perfectly. Population 400, good school, island doctor and nurse, even a football team, but most important of all it was on the east side of Orkney – absolutely vital for our intention of setting up a bird reserve on the island, and the habitat was perfect. Every garden seemed to overflow with the most beautiful fuchsia hedges – ideal for attracting migrant species in spring and autumn – and they were all small, no chasing shadows around these all day trying to glimpse the briefest view of any birds which may be skulking in the foliage. This was going to be birdwatching at its best!

And it certainly was! With such a wide diversity of habitat the island plays host to a wide variety of nesting species, the large seabird colonies towards the south of the island, the Skuas on the Rothiesholm headland where Red-throated Divers also nest, and

"This was going to be birdwatching at its best"
A male Red-backed Shrike close to one of the island post boxes in May 1977

the many wetlands in which up to ten species of duck breed including a large proportion of the British breeding population of Pintail.

Corncrakes too were still fairly wide-spread at the time and we had many sightings during that hot summer of 1977. But it was the migrants that we were really interested in. Without them we would have no hope of attracting visitors to the island.

9

A Glaucous Gull which took up residence just outside the house early in the new year and a party of 5 Jack Snipe feeding in the small pond behind the village street in early March got us off to a good start and we had several injured or sick birds brought to us by the locals, including a Turnstone which behaved in the same way as it would on a stony beach, flicking over the stones we had placed in one of our baking trays to hide the sand-hoppers put there for food. Several of these birds became amazingly tame and for much of our time in Whitehall Village the postman had to run the gauntlet of whatever birds happened to be in our conservatory when he delivered the mail.

Spring began well with all the common migrants one would expect in the north isles of Orkney – Redstarts, Pied Flycatchers, Blackcaps etc., – but where were the exotic species? Although we had little time for birdwatching during that spring we were beginning to feel slightly disappointed. Then in late May – 'Bang' – at least a dozen Red-backed Shrikes on the island! Stronsay had delivered! The previous day's maximum number recorded anywhere in Orkney was three and a 'phone call to Fair Isle that evening confirmed the huge arrival of the species in the northern isles – Fair Isle had recorded thirty!

The summer of 1977 was one of the best ever in Orkney and we had many 'phone calls from locals who knew we were interested in birds, alerting us to calling Corncrakes. Our patience was often rewarded and we managed to obtain good views of several of the birds from the roadside verges. Viewing was made particularly easy when calling birds appeared on low stone walls and began their rasping 'song' in the open.

Having spent several holidays on Fair Isle prior to moving to Orkney we knew the importance of easterly winds during migration. An easterly (anything between SE and NE) airflow across the North Sea generally brings large numbers of birds to the northern isles and as autumn approached we eagerly awaited the first arrivals. Almost on cue in mid-August the first birds began to appear and two Wrynecks and a Barred Warbler were found in the first garden we visited. An Icterine Warbler was also found along with good numbers of the more common species, all brought to Stronsay on an easterly wind.

Our first visitor not only saw many interesting birds during his stay with us but also had the good fortune to watch a school of nine Killer Whales passing the island off Lamb Head at the southern-most tip of the island. One of the 'pod' was an adult male.

August and September seem to be the best months for sightings of cetaceans and we now often see dolphins at this time of the year, particularly in Odiness Bay.

Ring Ouzel in mist. A typical late-autumn scene during mild easterly winds

More SE winds in mid-autumn brought a new variety of species to the island including Ring Ouzels and the first Redwings and Fieldfares, the new arrivals often perching on fence-posts as if to survey their new surroundings from a good vantage-point.

Then suddenly out of the blue came a 'phone call – "Would you be interested in running the Fair Isle shop?"

The chance was too good to turn down and after just over nine months on Stronsay during which time we had only scraped the surface ornithologically, we found ourselves on the Fair Isle boat 'Good Shepherd 111' heading NE for the remotest inhabited island in Britain.

*"Even the smallest yard can host
interesting species."
Flag-stone roofs and stone walls
are typical of the island's older buildings.
Many are still in daily use
and in excellent condition*

Stronsay 'first time around' had been a great experience and one thing we had learned is that migrants may turn up almost anywhere. Even the smallest yard can host interesting species. One such corner held a Blue Tit in late October (a real island rarity – Fair Isle recorded its first for 25 years during our time there) and a large garden plot of long tufty grass played host to our first island rarity – a Richard's Pipit, just two days before we set off for Fair Isle.

*This Richard's Pipit found at Lower Whitehall in October 1977
was our first island rarity, although the species is no longer on the list
considered by the British Birds Rarities Committee*

The Fair Isle Shop 'Stackhoull Stores' bathed in winter sunshine

Chapter 2

SIX YEARS ON FAIR ISLE

It's three miles long and one mile wide. Sheer cliffs over 500ft high rise majestically from the Atlantic, and sixty or so islanders brave the elements there year in year out. And yet what many of the visitors who go to the island are looking for is less than five inches long and hides in ditches – the Lanceolated Warbler!

Well it is Fair Isle and birdwatchers are like that!

Of course it is much easier to get there nowadays with several planes a week and a 70ft boat – quite a different story back in the sixties! Then the only transport was the 50ft 'Good Shepherd II' and the 25 mile journey from Shetland could be interesting to say the least. There are stories of holidaymakers travelling all the way up from the south and on seeing the island ferry refusing to go on it and thereby missing their holiday. Others have watched the boat loading up at Grutness pier at the south end of Shetland mainland, waved to the crew as they set off on the journey back to Fair Isle, and an hour or so later discovered that they too should have been on the boat. They had not even considered that such a small boat could possibly be the ferry!

Since the early seventies life on Fair Isle has changed considerably. There is now an island water supply, an aero-generator supplying much of the island's electricity and of course a regular air-service from Shetland. This has resulted in a more stable population, a far cry from the fifties when de-population seemed imminent.

We arrived on the isle in 1977, a few months before the island water-supply was connected, and enjoyed coffee-coloured bath water (due to the peat in our old supply) and fresh-water shrimps from the cold tap. A great experience, and did it worry us? Not a bit.

Much of our spare time during our first year was spent building up walls and redesigning the garden in order to attract the birds to us rather than us go chasing them. This worked so well that by the time we left the isle in 1983 the shop garden had become the place for certain species. Marsh, Icterine and Barred Warblers made good use of the rose bushes, and Common Rosefinches joined in at the corn with the local sparrows. Most of our Fair Isle sightings are documented in 'Fair Isle's Garden Birds' published by The Shetland Times in 1984.

Running the shop was a great experience and we were well patronised by the whole community including the Bird Observatory. But there were extremes! In appalling weather there may be whole days without a single customer and others when it seemed that the whole island had come shopping. We may come home from a dance at midnight to find the crew of a fishing-boat waiting patiently for us in the hope that we would serve them – we always did of course – and there may be times during migration when all the visitors seemed to have disappeared – we knew then that a mega-rarity was on the isle somewhere!

Life on Fair Isle was always interesting – winds up to 150mph, so violent that large fish were literally thrown out of the raging sea and onto the beach; beautiful aurora lighting the whole sky, including one of the best in living memory which could be heard 'hissing' its pulsating rhythm as we watched the magnificent display of colours in total awe; huge arrivals of autumn migrants when the whole isle seemed alive with birds, and those 'red-letter' days when, from out of the blue, a totally unexpected rarity would turn up. The white Gyrfalcon flying over the garden in December 1982 was such an event. Similarly a Short-toed Lark landing – albeit briefly – in the front garden; an Olive-backed pipit striding around the long grass in the back garden and a Water Rail found nestled among the eggs in the hen-house were all totally unexpected.

A winter view from the Fair Isle shop –
a scene rarely witnessed by visitors to the island

With the lack of diversity of habitat on Fair Isle many species turn up in areas one would not normally find them and there are many amazing records of rarities being found in the most unexpected places. A White's Thrush in one of the war-time buildings at Lower Station on Ward Hill; a Greenish Warbler in an out-house at the North Lighthouse, and the Roller we found resting on a wall at the rear of the shop are all examples of what in the Northern Isles is almost the norm. The Roller was the first record of the species on Fair Isle as was the Red Kite which drifted slowly north over us in January 1979 – long before the recent reintroduction scheme which now blurs the picture of genuine wild bird sightings.

15

Just how many birds fail to make land-fall during migration can only be guessed at, but when one witnesses huge 'falls' during high winds on what is virtually a speck in the ocean, it would seem inevitable that large numbers perish at sea.

Although we tend to talk of bird 'sightings' the Spring of 1983 on Fair Isle was most noticeable for the number of species 'in song'. An incredible variety were heard singing around the shop – and all species that do not nest on the isle! These included Black Redstart, Ring Ouzel, Brambling, Dunnock, Whitethroat, Blackcap and Willow Warbler. A Marsh Warbler spent a whole day singing in our roses in the front garden and elsewhere on the isle Song Thrush, Sedge Warbler and Common Rosefinch were heard.

The Roller of September 1981. A new bird for Fair Isle

The most amazing however was the Wood Warbler which we watched parachuting down onto our garden fence whilst trilling its beautiful song – and not a tree in sight!

So just where are the best places to look for birds on Fair Isle? The answer to that is "Anywhere!" Very few of the migrant species would choose the type of habitat they encounter when arriving on the island and many use whatever shelter is available in order to rest and feed. The west cliffs are sometimes teeming with birds during autumn 'falls' although there is a tendency among visiting birdwatchers to concentrate their efforts around the crofts. Some species appear to prefer the shelter and vertical plane of the cliffs whilst others such as Bluethroats are often found in ditches close to the crofts.

"Bluethroats are often found in ditches"

Goldcrests certainly seem to prefer the short-cropped grass areas along the cliff edges and were comparatively rare in the garden. The roses we planted held no attraction for them at all.

Some species are fairly predictable even though they are in the 'wrong' habitat. Crossbills when present are often found above the cliff-face at Hoillie close to the Bird Observatory; Golden Orioles are generally found feeding among the heather – although there is a lot of it, and Red-breasted Flycatchers are most likely to be found in the geos and on the cliffs rather than around the crofts.

Other species however are totally unpredictable and may turn up just about anywhere on the isle. The Red-flanked Blue-tail of 1981 was found feeding on a pile of newly-cut turf at a

The Red-flanked Bluetail of 1981

17

building-site and yet the following day it was discovered two miles away feeding along the edge of the North Haven beach. I have found Rustic Buntings on the top of Ward Hill – at over seven hundred feet the highest point on the isle; in the vegetable garden and in stubble fields; Richard's Pipits along cliff edges in short-cropped grass, feeding in the road, and even on a tarred shed roof, and Pallas's Warblers in gardens – sadly not our own, on cliff-sides, and in the tiny area of spruce trees known as 'The Plantation'.

There is also a long list of species which have been discovered 'self-caught' in one or other of the Heligoland traps. These include such unlikely species as Richard's Pipit, Hoopoe and River Warbler.

The luckiest sighting during our stay on the isle occurred in June 1981. A middle-aged couple had gone to the North Lighthouse area to look for Puffins and as they sat looking over the cliff-edge there, discovered an Alpine Swift hawking along the cliff-face just a few feet below them. What was so lucky about their find was the fact that the bird had been seen earlier in the day near the South end of the isle by a foreign visitor who did not realise that the bird was so rare in Great Britain and had only casually mentioned the bird over lunch. That afternoon virtually everyone from the observatory was scanning the skies in the hope of relocating the bird and yet it was discovered by the only people who were not actually looking for it!

One of the Fair Isle 'specialities' – Yellow-breasted Bunting – is very predictable in its choice of habitat, being almost invariably found in the standing oat crops. One very dull individual was discovered in 1992 by an island visitor who put into practise my suggestion in 'Fair Isle's Garden Birds' for those visitors hoping to find the species, i.e. – "Come to Fair Isle in September, select one of the fields of corn (oats) and sit and watch it while praying for south-east winds!" It certainly worked for him – on his very first day on the isle – and what could well have been the same bird turned up on Stronsay the day after it was last seen on Fair Isle.

It is interesting to note that the Cretzschmar's Bunting found in June 1979 spent most of its stay in a field of newly sown oats.

It is not unusual for visiting birdwatchers to fall into the 'It's

Fair Isle so it must be a rarity' trap. It could be called 'geographical twitching' and I have seen very experienced ornithologists literally jump on hearing the perfectly ordinary call of a Meadow Pipit. No doubt they would have no bother with the identification on 'home territory' – but on Fair Isle it just might be ....!

Of course it is all relative. What may be a super-rarity in the south of England can be annual in the northern isles. Many Common Rosefinches visited our garden during our time on Fair Isle and yet there are very few records of the species from my home county of Kent. Similarly Blue Tits, common in the south are extremely rare in the northern isles and I well remember how many birders dashed to the North Lighthouse to see Fair Isle's first record of the species for 25 years!

It was the well-known pioneer of British ornithology Eagle Clarke who first realised the importance of Fair Isle for studying migration and he made several subsequent visits to the isle after his initial five-week stay there in the autumn of 1905.

Whilst flicking through a pile of old books we purchased at a house sale on the isle in the early eighties I came across a postcard

dated 'Xmas 1908'. It read – "With Best Wishes to all at Stoneybreck from Mr Eagle Clarke". A real treasure which holds pride of place in our book-case along with the two-volume 'Studies in Bird Migration' written by Eagle Clarke and published in 1912.

Surgeon Rear-admiral Stenhouse was another pioneer ornithologist from earlier this century, and the Duchess of Bedford who stayed in the house now known as 'Pund' also contributed much to the study of migration. Pund was in fact formerly known as 'Ortolan Cottage' reflecting the ornithological connection.

Although there is very little cover on the isle and the birds are therefore generally easy to find and study, Fair Isle can and does present problems to the unwary. Judging the size of birds can be difficult as the sheer magnitude of the cliffs dwarfs many migrant species, giving a false impression of their size. Colour too can be difficult to judge where birds are in the 'wrong' habitat. This applies particularly to species such as Marsh and Reed Warblers, and although trapping and in-the-hand examination has resolved many controversies over the identification of particular birds, even this can present problems. Birds in the hand and in false light can appear totally different to their general appearance in the field.

When we left Fair Isle in October 1983 to return to our home-town of Gillingham it was with very mixed feelings. We would certainly miss the freedom and life-style but we were looking forward to finding the right place on Stronsay and setting up the reserve, as we had intended back in 1977.

Lanceolated Warbler – almost 'reptilian' in appearance. THE Fair Isle speciality!

The Medway estuary at Gillingham, looking north
towards Kingsnorth Power Station. Nor Marsh is to the right

Chapter 3

BACK ON THE 'LOCAL PATCH'

It could have been a huge anti-climax – but it wasn't! We had been thoroughly spoilt on Fair Isle with such an array of exotic species on our 'local patch' at Stackhoull Stores, and the 'old home town' of Gillingham on the south bank of the river Medway could hardly be expected to provide such ornithological delights. But again it is all relative, and although we did not see the rarities, there were a number of memorable sightings during our four years back in Kent after leaving Fair Isle, including Pomarine and Arctic Skuas flying right over our cottage. We often wonder if any of the latter species were birds we had seen on Fair Isle during our time there.

What we found most encouraging on our return was the huge upsurge in interest in the environment, and the borough council's plans for a major Country Park along the southern shore of the Medway.

I had been responsible for some of the early work in setting up the park in the mid-seventies during my time working for the local authority there. Riverside Country Park as it is now known is one of Kent's major attractions and is a shining example of what can be achieved by a local council. The council's nearby off-shore island of Nor Marsh is now an R.S.P.B. reserve and internationally important for wintering wildfowl and waders. It can be viewed from the inaptly named 'Horrid Hill' which has itself played host to many interesting species including Wrynecks and shrikes, and I shall never forget the thrill of finding a magnificent Great Grey Shrike perched proudly on top of the very end bush of the narrow half-mile long causeway to Horrid Hill – still without doubt the most memorable 'find' I ever made on what was for over two decades my 'local patch'.

On returning to Gillingham from Fair Isle in 1983 I soon found myself back in my old job running the local outdoor swimming pool on the south shore of the Medway close to Chatham Dockyard – again ideally situated for studying migration – when there were no customers! Over the years there I had previously seen many interesting species – parties of Arctic Skuas wheeling above the swimming pool before flying off inland and presumably right across Kent to the south coast some forty miles away; flocks of up to 90 Black Terns storm-driven into the estuary where they would feed in the river immediately outside the pool, and flocks of waders – in particular Whimbrel – heading off south, driven from the mud-flats by the rising tide. The swimming pool itself hosted many interesting species over the years including Moorhens in the footbaths and Grey Wagtails feeding around the edge in winter. Osprey and Serin were both seen flying over.

I enjoyed a host of interesting bird sightings during the two mile walk to work along the estuary, including Wrynecks, Red-backed Shrikes, Redstarts, Whinchats and Pied Flycatchers. On the estuary itself Little Egret, Avocet and even a Manx Shearwater were seen – the latter completely lost at low tide! (A dowitcher seen here in October 1976 defied specific identification but could well have been Britain's first ever Short-billed.)

Probably the most surprising sight however was of a party of four Bearded Tits in the tiny reedy ditch at the western edge of the country park, a species I dreamed of seeing there one day when I used to birdwatch in the area as a boy.

The Pomarine Skua which flew over our cottage in late autumn was probably the most unexpected bird we recorded from the house, but the children often saw Barn Owls from the bedroom windows and we recorded five species of bat including Long-eared which we would often see picking moths from the top of the dam-son hedge at the end of the garden. A small flock of Goosander flew west over the house during the huge snow-fall in January 1987 when three feet of level snow fell over a single weekend

More snow fell in one weekend in Kent than in the whole of our fifteen years in the northern isles!

The Medway estuary as a whole is internationally important as a wintering area for wildfowl and waders and many of these spend the winter within the Gillingham Borough boundary around Nor Marsh and Motney Hill. It is to the council's credit that great strides have been taken to help preserve these areas. Flocks of Avocets are now seen regularly in winter and many breeding species have a secure future, a far cry from last century when Prentis, in his book 'The Birds of Rainham' (Kent) stated that ... "Generally in the Medway are to be found more craft than birds."

Many rare birds were recorded along the Medway during the last century however and Prentis himself accumulated a comprehensive collection of stuffed birds from the area. Some of these are still on display in Rochester Museum and the 'Prentis Collection' as it is known was very useful when compiling 'The Birds of Gillingham' in 1984.

We had enjoyed our time back in Gillingham but out of the blue in 1987 we found the ideal site for our reserve on Stronsay. By early autumn that year we found ourselves heading north once again!

Great Grey Shrike. An exciting find on any local patch

"View from the Reserve, looking south-east across Mill Bay"

Chapter 4

RETURN TO STRONSAY

We needed a target. Having found the perfect spot alongside the two miles of golden sand at Mill Bay on the east side of Stronsay, we had to have a target. Setting up a Bird Reserve specifically to attract migrants is all very well but how would we know if we had been successful?

It did not take long to decide. Fair Isle is just forty miles away and there are a number of species which turn up there regularly and yet are extremely rare elsewhere in the U.K. It had to be one of them, and as we intended to sow small areas of oats for seed-eating species there really was no contest – it had to be Yellow-breasted Bunting. Fair Isle has long been the place to see the species, and during our six years there we saw several, all but one in the standing oat crops.

The decision had been made and each subsequent autumn we held our breath, hoping that we had not after all been over optimistic. As each year passed the list of birds recorded on the Reserve grew and included several species of bunting, but still no sign of the one we had set our hearts on. And then in September '92, there in the very patch of oats we had planted for it was our very own Yellow-breasted Bunting. It had all been worthwhile!

We had taken a big chance coming to Stronsay. Apart from ourselves in 1977 and a few day-trippers before and since, the island was relatively unwatched, and compared to Fair Isle it is big! But we held on to our belief that if Fair Isle gets the birds then so must Stronsay, and being able to see the former from our roof on clear days was an incentive from the outset.

Arriving back on the island in 1987 Stronsay was once again our 'local patch'. In our home town of Gillingham we had always been advocates of 'local patch birding', hardly ever wandering from the shores of the Medway to birdwatch. It is most encouraging that this approach to ornithology has mushroomed in recent years – just imagine what birds would be discovered if we all concentrated our efforts on our own local patches! Of course not everyone is lucky enough to have a Stronsay on the doorstep so it is not surprising that many keen birdwatchers head for the traditional sites such as Cley or Dungeness. 'Local patch' birding however could turn out to be one of the most valuable assets for pressure-groups on matters of local planning etc. and should be encouraged by all with an interest in the environment.

Our own 'local patch' was to be the five acres we had purchased at 'Milltown' where the two-hundred year old house known as 'The Castle' stood in glorious dereliction. It had not been lived-in for almost twenty years and yet the main part of the house was amazingly dry, and by Spring 1988 all the repairs and renovation work was complete and we were ready for action. The garden walls were all rebuilt and we added several others as shelter for the many trees and shrubs we were to plant over the coming years, all designed of course with the intention of providing cover for as wide a variety of migrant species as possible. One large area we had ear-marked for vegetables was immediately covered in a sheet of black polythene to kill off the weeds and it was this area which attracted our first garden rarity not long after we had moved in – an immaculate Arctic Redpoll.

There was certainly no doubt about this birds identity, it was a stunning 'hornemannii'.

" 'The Castle' stood in glorious dereliction"

It spent virtually the whole of its several-day stay with us feeding on nettle seeds which had fallen onto the polythene from around the edge of the garden, and although perhaps not the ideal setting for such a beautiful species the black of the polythene contrasted perfectly with the whiteness of the bird's plumage.

Ornithologically much had happened during our first year back on Stronsay although much of this time was taken up with habitat creation. We had however managed to fit in some bird watching, and the gardens – which had been one of the main attractions that brought us to the island – had proved their value instantly. Early Wrynecks and Icterine Warblers were seen and as we approached the garden at Holin Cottage one day in late September our first Yellow-browed Warbler flitted out and into view.

At least six Richard's Pipits were seen during the autumn of 1987 and it is interesting that all were first located in the road rather than in what is generally accepted as their preferred habitat i.e long grass. Although I had seen newly arrived birds of the species on the road during our time on Fair Isle they seemed to rapidly filter into areas of often long grass. However, having had the opportunity to study the Stronsay birds for long periods without any disturbance it soon became clear that they appeared to prefer to feed in the dry road rather than in the fields alongside. I watched many of the birds taking worms and other food from the edge of the verges where the vegetation overhung the dry tarmac, and whilst watching them it suddenly clicked – there was no traffic for sometimes hours on end on the side-roads where most of the birds were first seen and these birds seemed quite content to feed in the manner of Pied Wagtails on the tarmac. Birds first found on the busier roads however were soon flushed into the surrounding grassy fields as happens to the Fair Isle birds, where in general the

Arctic Redpoll on the Reserve

roads are far busier than the Stronsay roads during migration due to the number of pedestrians. This leads to a false impression of the species' preferred habitat.

Other species which were recorded in good numbers in autumn 1987 were Lapland Buntings – including a party of four feeding among silage just outside our garden; Ring Ouzels and Redstarts, and there were sightings of Chiffchaffs right up until Christmas. A Tree-creeper was seen working its way round one of the high stone chimney-stacks in Whitehall Village in its desperate search for food, and on the 21st October during a big 'fall' of migrants our first 'BB' rarity was found feeding in a farm track – a beautiful Rustic Bunting.

Rustic Bunting – our first island rarity

Sandwich Terns were seen into November and although the Orkney breeding colonies of the species are the most northerly in Europe we discovered small numbers wintering around the isle during several subsequent years. All the more astonishing considering that the vast majority of the British breeding population winters off the coast of Africa.

The most striking bird of 1987 however was not a rarity or even uncommon. It was a leucistic-type Reed Bunting which from a distance could be mistaken for a Canary. There was a suggestion of typical female Reed Bunting's head-pattern but the plumage was

The most striking bird of 1987 was this 'leucistic-type' Reed Bunting

basically yellow fading to white on the flight-feathers. The bird was a real beauty but we wondered how long it would take before one of the many wintering Merlins plucked it from the ditch near 'Airy' where it spent most of its time among the small flock of its normal-coloured relatives who all seemed to accept it as one of them. It was heard to give the typical call of the species on several occasions and was last seen in March 1988 – so had at least survived the winter.

One of the most encouraging aspects of the year was that as we had suspected, the gardens were great attractions to many species, which made finding them on such a relatively big island – the size of 4 Fair Isles – that bit easier, and as the gardens are generally a considerable distance apart, birds are reluctant to leave the cover of the one they are in which again helps in relocating species after the initial sighting. On islands with large areas of cover, relocating birds can be extremely frustrating and time-consuming!

As is often the case with cetacean corpses, a Common Porpoise

A Common Porpoise washed ashore in autumn 1987

washed ashore in autumn 1987 bore the scars of encounters with other sea-mammals. Although initially disturbing, the occasional sighting of a dead porpoise etc. possibly indicates a healthy population in the area.

Since 1987 we have seen several species of cetacean including many which we could not specifically identify, the best views being of a school of Pilot Whales in May 1988 and a small school of White-beaked Dolphins in 1993. The dolphins appeared to be 'playing' with one of their young, tossing it out of the water on several occasions close inshore in St Catherine's Bay. A school of dolphins were rescued in the bay that year after 'beaching' on the sand.

There are populations of both Common and Grey seals around the island and these can often be found 'hauled-out' on the rocks and quiet beaches. One small beach close to the road near Whitehall Village has been a favourite site for Common Seals for generations. Numbers of both species seem to be fairly constant and fortunately the virus which killed large numbers of seals over much of eastern Britain in the late eighties did not reach as far north as Stronsay.

1987 had been a great success and we were looking forward to moving into the newly-renovated house 'Castle' in spring of the following year.

*"The first garden we looked in held Wryneck, 4 Pied Flycatchers
and several species of warbler"*

1988

Little did we realise as we scanned the flock of 43 Corn Buntings feeding near the Kirk on 2nd January 1988 that not only was it a large proportion of the entire Orkney population but that in seven years time it would have dwindled to just one individual.

In the late eighties Stronsay still held a dozen or so pairs, but in common with the rest of Britain numbers have been declining steadily for many years. We had hopes of attracting a pair to breed on the Reserve and birds have been present for a time in spring on several occasions, attracted to the oat stubble on which they were feeding, but although we have had singing birds in the area, breeding has not been proved and the chance may now have gone. On the 'plus' side Curlews are now common breeding birds whereas even twenty years ago they were rare.

Another 'plus' is the increase in the number of waders and wildfowl during the winter months, with the Meikle Water alone playing host to thousands of duck and a party of White-fronted Geese. Whenever a Peregrine is in the vicinity the sky is absolutely alive with waders and duck which can make finding the falcon very difficult at times. This was never illustrated more vividly than in April 1994 when the birds around the loch seemed even more disturbed than when Peregrines fly over, and it was pure good fortune that we discovered that the culprit was a beautiful white Gyrfalcon!

The spring of 1988 was amazing! There had been early records of Chiffchaff, Wheatear, Black Redstart and a superb male Lapland Bunting – all before the end of March. The turning-circle just outside the house was by now complete and had been built up with mounds of stone and earth to create an area which has since attracted several species of British rarities as a result of the wild-flowers and weeds we have cultivated there.

March and April had been excellent for migrants but it is May 1988 that will long live in our memory. Our sightings that month included a male Subalpine Warbler and a school of Pilot Whales close inshore near Whitehall.

It began on Friday the 13th! Suddenly there were birds everywhere, and it was warm. The first garden we visited held Red-backed Shrike, Pied and Spotted Flycatchers, four species of warbler, and a Black Redstart – none of which breed on Stronsay. Several other migrant species were recorded that day including Whinchats and Redstarts, but the most encouraging sign was the

Subalpine Warbler – just a few yards from a singing Bluethroat!

presence of Tree Pipits and Wood Warblers – both excellent 'indicator' species in the northern isles. Their presence usually indicates a big influx of birds of many species and this has been proved to be right time and time again.

The next two days were even better with at least 10 Red-backed Shrikes and 4 brilliant male Bluethroats, the highlight being the male Subalpine Warbler found in one of the island ditches just a few yards from where one of the Bluethroats was singing. Another 'BB' rarity – and again we had found it ourselves.

Although only present for one day the Subalpine Warbler gave us breathtaking views as it occasionally perched out in the open on top of the large flagstones which border the ditch in which it was found.

By late May migration is virtually over in the south of Great Britain, but not so in Orkney. The end of May and early June is generally the best time to look for rarities, particularly over-shooting birds from southern Europe and late migrants heading for Scandinavia and elsewhere in northern Europe. Birdwatching at this time of year however can be exhausting – with 20 hours of daylight there is the temptation to be out 'in the field' for as long as possible!

The hot weather of mid-May 1988 continued, and although we had never seriously considered the likelihood of ever finding a species new for Orkney we were soon to experience the joy of such an event.

We had recently purchased a 1933 Morris Ten car and set off to see if any new migrants had arrived on the 27th May. Little did we know that we were about to discover the benefit of 'old' technology!

As we rounded the bend near Holin Cottage a small bird rose up from the edge of the road and flew directly away from the car just a few feet above the centre of the road. It looked very pale and sandy-coloured and my immediate thoughts went to Short-toed Lark – one of the typical, late-spring overshooting species. But as it landed in the road about fifty yards away I could see that it had a long tail and high horizontal stance – a Tawny Pipit.

This was where the 'old' technology came into its own! I managed to manoeuvre the car to within twenty yards of the bird and not

1933 Morris 10/4 - excellent for birdwatching!

only enjoyed brilliant views of it through the flat glass windscreen but also obtained photographs as it stood in the road. The sloping windscreen of a modern car would have made observation difficult and photography impossible but the flat windscreen of the 1933 Morris was ideal for both with no distortion at all. The fact that we obtain such excellent views through the windscreen means that we do not have to position the car in order to wind down the side windows for viewing, a practise that often results in the rapid departure of the quarry.

The Tawny Pipit was one of those classic overshooting species and the date absolutely typical. It is also interesting that this bird like many of the closely related Richard's Pipits we have seen here, was also found feeding in the road although the surrounding habitat was ideal, being short grass and dunes on the shore of Mill Bay.

The old Morris has proved invaluable over the years and is still giving excellent service, and although we, like most nature-lovers prefer to be out in the open air, the use of a car as a temporary hide

Tawny Pipit – the first record for Orkney

brings amazing results and many of the birds we have discovered whilst driving slowly past the island ditches and gardens would have been missed if we had been on foot. A car is particularly useful during what is generally the best conditions for big 'falls' – southeast winds and drizzle.

Within an hour of finding the Tawny Pipit we discovered a red singing male Common Rosefinch and a female nearby, both feeding on dandelions on the roadside verge and again both photographed from the car.

At this time of year the island is at its best, the cattle are grazing in the lush meadows and there is generally an air of peace and

"There is generally an air of peace and tranquillity around the farm buildings"

tranquillity around the farm buildings. Day after day we enjoyed blue skies and magnificent sunsets and we often found ourselves outside working in the garden until almost midnight. It is very easy to lose track of time during the summer months at such latitudes!

Stronsay is known as 'The Island of Three Bays' and there are magnificent views looking west towards the other Orkney islands. During the long summer twilight the whole scene can be washed with the most delicate pink hue when all that can be heard are the cries of sea-birds. The view from Bomasty Bay is particularly beautiful and the Stronsay School too enjoys breath-taking views across much of Orkney.

A summer sunset at Bomasty Bay

6 Red-backed Shrikes and 2 Icterine Warblers at the very end of May were accompanied by a whole range of common species and we had high hopes of finding one of the northern isles specialities during the first week of June – Marsh Warbler. Although not a rarity in the true sense of the word it is a rare breeding species in the U.K. and very, difficult to observe in its natural habitat on the breeding grounds. Quite a different story on Stronsay where the species is very predictable in its timing and choice of habitat. Most of those seen on the island have been found singing in one or other of the gardens, giving excellent views and the opportunity to study all the features at close range.

By the second of June we had one! As we stepped out of the car to check one of the island gardens we were greeted by the beautiful rich song of a Marsh Warbler from the fuchsia hedge there. As is usual with this species the song contained much mimicry of other bird-song and this one had immediately 'tuned-in' to the local Linnets and was copying much of their song to perfection.

The hot spell of 1988 continued and we were treated to both Corncrake and Quail calling in one of the fields adjacent to the Reserve although there was no proof of breeding. We decided to leave the birds in peace rather than risk disturbing them.

There was an excellent passage of waders during the summer of 1988 and Garganey were seen on many occasions giving rise to the possibility that no less than ten species of duck may have nested on the island that year! A quite phenomenal number.

Mid-August was warm and sunny and there had been no sign of passerine migrants at all as we went on a social visit to a nearby farm. A small warbler flitted out of the garden there and we almost passed it off as a Willow Warbler as it disappeared into the adjoining yard. I decided to go and have a look – just in case – and as I raised my binoculars I could see that the bird had pure white underparts – and yes, a distinct neat white wing-bar! There was no doubt – it was a Greenish Warbler, only the third ever seen in Orkney.

As if to confirm my identification the bird went straight back into the garden and began singing from the top of the fuchsia hedge in and around which it spent much of its four-day stay on the island. On the way home from the farm that evening we saw just one other small migrant – a Barred Warbler, making a quite amazing opening duo of the autumn migration.

A second Greenish Warbler was found two days later on the 18th at Mount Pleasant some four miles away but just in case it was the same bird we dashed back to the site of the first bird and were delighted to find it was still there. A big relief – 2 in a year is almost unbelievable and yet we were to end the autumn with no less than four sightings of the species, three of which we managed to photograph. With much doubt hanging over some of the British records of this species it was vital that we obtained photographic evidence of our birds, after all, who would believe four on an unknown island? Fair Isle perhaps – but Stronsay?!!

Our first American 'vagrant' was found on the 18th August at 'Dale'.

Whilst scanning across a flock of 400 Golden Plover in a field there, I was suddenly aware of a very grey-looking bird somewhat detached from the main flock. Fortunately it was the nearest bird to the road and I was able to study it at close range from the car for prolonged periods. It proved to be a 'Lesser' Golden Plover of the American sub-species 'dominica' – the first record of the species in Orkney this century and only the second ever.

Our first American species – a 'Lesser' Golden Plover

The 2nd September 1988 was without doubt the best day's bird watching I have ever known.

The 1st was clear and dry and there were very few migrant passerines on the isle, but as we watched the weather forecast that evening our minds began to race. A depression was moving up the North Sea bringing strong SE winds and rain straight towards us – perfect conditions for a big 'fall' of continental migrants. Any birds moving south over the area that night would run straight into the front.

We lay in bed that night listening to the high wind and rain on the windows imagining what we might see the next day, but we had no idea just how good the 2nd would turn out to be.

A quite amazing fall had occurred and a quick look out of the kitchen window revealed Pied Flycatcher, Blackcap, Garden Warbler and Tree Pipit – that excellent indicator species!

Within five minutes we were on our way and as we set off along

One of an amazing four Greenish Warblers recorded on Stronsay in 1988

the road we could hear Tree Pipits calling, and birds seemed to be literally dropping out of the sky.

The first garden we visited held Wryneck, 4 Pied Flycatchers and several species of warbler including Barred. At the first farm we found a Greenish Warbler, at least 2 Ortolans, Red-backed Shrike and Wryneck, along with dozens of other migrants of more common species. The bushes and ditches were alive with warblers and flycatchers and ornithologically it was actually funny! Everywhere we looked there were birds, and the number we missed that day can only be guessed at but was without doubt more than we actually saw as we did not manage to cover even half the island! We seemed to spend half the day writing down birds we had seen, and we were in 'the field' from dawn until dusk. There appeared to be Whinchats on every fence and many birds went unidentified as

Barred Warbler, a regular autumn 'semi-rarity'

we simply did not have time to try to relocate the dozens which flew away from the shelter of the farm buildings and gardens as we approached.

Some of the totals recorded that day were amazing:– 66 Whinchats, 60 Willow Warblers, 37 Pied Flycatchers, 23 Garden Warblers, 20 Tree Pipits, 14 Redstarts, 6 Red-backed Shrikes, 6 Wrynecks, 4 Wood Warblers, 2 Barred Warblers, 2 Greenish Warblers, and at least 2 Ortolans – a memorable day!

As most of the migrants which turn up in the autumn are tired, hungry and probably lost, it is not surprising that they are often

Such corners provide vital shelter for many species

found in the most unlikely places. Woodland species in particular look very out of place as they search for food along the stone walls and among old farm machinery, but it is here that the insects are most likely to be found. We now have several favourite corners scattered around the island that provide food and shelter for such species and are absolutely vital for their survival.

Of the five Yellow-browed Warblers which arrived on the island in early October 1988, 3 were found in gardens, 2 in roadside ditches and 1 in a patch of roadside nettles showing yet again the unpredictability of where migrants are likely to occur.

The autumn continued with several sightings of Long-tailed Skuas – all adults – including one which took up residence in Mill Bay for a few days. We could often see this bird from the garden as it chased the local terns and gulls, and as is often the case with birds of this species in the northern isles in the autumn it looked lost and rather aimless in its behaviour.

There was another amazing run of rare and uncommon species starting on the 10th October, and although not quite so dramatic as the fall of 2nd September, wave after wave of migrants arrived from the continent. 3 Bluethroats, 2 Richard's Pipits, 3 Rosefinches and several more Yellow-browed Warblers were seen including our first of the latter species for the Reserve where it fed among the nettles close to the shore. These were all however totally eclipsed by a Radde's Warbler – Orkney's 3rd – on the 13th, and a very obliging Pied Wheatear on the 16th.

The Radde's Warbler was again found in a dense garden and gave excellent views as it fed on the ground below the fuchsia hedge. Once again, with no pressure on the bird, we had ideal opportunities

One of three Bluethroats found in the same ditch during October

Pied Wheatear – almost hidden on the rocky beach

to study it at close quarters.

The bird called frequently – a nervous "teck teck", much softer than the rather harsh "tack" call of the similar Dusky Warbler. It was seen in flight on several occasions when the undertail coverts and flank colouration gave the bird a rather 'brownish' appearance when viewed from below. This could partly account for some past controversies over the identification of the species elsewhere in the U.K. when views have been brief.

The Pied Wheatear was a great find for one of our first paying guests at the reserve. It was discovered feeding just above the beach at 'The Pow' at the south end of the island and was present for several days. A probable first-year female it presented us with the most difficult identification problem within the Wheatear group, but again this bird was so obliging that we were able to study it at very close range for prolonged periods.

It often used the tall weeds and debris in the area from which it would fly down to pluck flies from the beach below.

The bird had a generally more horizontal carriage than the common

Radde's Warbler – yet another rare species found in an island garden!

Wheatear and there was considerably more white on the back and tail. The bill was rather fine and in general the bird appeared rather more delicate than that species.

Fortunately we managed to obtain a series of excellent photographs of the bird, which not only confirmed our identification but also helped to get the record accepted by the British Birds Rarities Committee. Only the second ever seen in Orkney, the first being on Swona on the 1st November 1916.

The day after the Pied Wheatear was found, the same visitor discovered our first island Red-breasted Flycatcher, way out on the very end of the Odiness peninsula. This bird too was using tall weeds as vantage points in its search for food.

Pied Wheatear – a great find for one of our first visitors

The last few days of October 1988 were notable for the range of species present including Long and Short-eared Owls. Surprisingly, several species of warbler were still present and there were good numbers of migrant finches – mainly Brambling and Chaffinches, another Common Rosefinch, and our one and only record of Goosander for the island, a male flying past the Reserve on the 24th.

There was then a welcome lull until the immaculate Arctic Redpoll in the Reserve garden from the 5th-7th November, and the month ended with a first-winter Pomarine Skua present in The Pow area where it could often be seen harassing gulls.

A fantastic first year – Stronsay had delivered the goods!

The 'White Slaps' gateway at Whitehall Farm. A unique island feature

The Bird Reserve was officially opened in August 1989

1989

1988 had been an amazing year and 1989 had yet more surprises in store.

The year had hardly begun when we were given a reminder of how mild the winters can be in Orkney with the sight of a Chiffchaff feeding among the weeds on the turning circle, whilst on the beach below the house 2 wintering Sandwich Terns consorted with an Iceland Gull – a strange association in the U.K.

With its irregular coastline and deeply indented bays, nowhere on the island is more than a mile from the sea and as a consequence frosts are very rare, four or five a year being about average. There has been little snow for over a decade and although there have been several hurricanes with winds over 100mph since we came to Stronsay, the temperature during the winter averages close to that in Kent – and without the extreme lows encountered in the SE of England. It is therefore not surprising that most years Chiffchaffs attempt to winter in Orkney.

Why Sandwich Terns winter in Orkney however is a complete mystery. Most of the British breeding population winter off the

46

coast of Africa and with the Stronsay breeding birds being virtually the most northerly in the world it is even more incredible that a few have remained throughout the winter in recent years. It is of course impossible to be sure that the wintering birds are the same birds which breed on the island and it may be that they are not local birds at all, as an individual which wintered off the coast of Holland some years ago was trapped and found to be carrying an American ring – a totally unexpected and unprecedented occurrence.

Much of our time in 1989 was spent creating new habitat on the Reserve and we were encouraged in our work when the Nature Conservancy Council (now Scottish Natural Heritage) offered a grant towards planting and sowing. From the outset it was our intention to use only those species endemic to Orkney and we have stuck rigidly to this approach although there have been dilemmas. Most gardens on the island are adorned with beautiful fuchsia hedges – a South American species, as is the hebe (local name Veronica), both introduced into the island last century, probably by whalers returning from the South Atlantic, (Stronsay had strong links with the whaling industry about this time). Deciding that they were both now well established enough to be called 'naturalised' at least, we decided to plant several of both species in 1989 and just hope that one day they attain the size and magnificence of many of those elsewhere on the island. Not only are they vital for migrants and certain nesting species they add a welcome splash of colour to what would otherwise be a rather bleak landscape, flowering virtually throughout the year.

Two totally unexpected birds were seen in March that year – a Goldfinch on the Reserve and a Blue Tit in Whitehall Village. Both are extreme rarities in the northern isles but unlike many such species these two were found in ideal habitat – the Goldfinch feeding on thistles and the Blue Tit feeding at a bird-table.

More exotic species were in store however starting with a Great Grey Shrike which spent a day on the Reserve in late April and a Golden Oriole which was seen by many people on the island – but not ourselves! This latter bird illustrated perfectly just how difficult some species can be to relocate in the northern isles. As with Fair Isle, Golden Orioles on Stronsay are generally found feeding on the ground and as there are close on 1,000 fields on the island it is hardly surprising that we could not relocate it in spite of much searching!

There was a huge sudden movement of terns on the evening of 5th May 1989. Small parties were passing northwards across the island, emerging from the SW corner of Mill Bay and flying past the Reserve on their journey to breeding grounds further north. Most were Arctic Terns but there were a number of Common Terns also, generally in separate groups. It soon became very easy to identify most of the birds as they were virtually all in breeding plumage, the longer streamers of the Arctics being very noticeable. Hundreds passed northwards during the evening and having just seen a small party of the more 'stocky-looking' Common Terns followed closely by a group of the more 'streamlined' Arctics a single very white-looking bird caught my eye directly behind them. Its tail streamers were even longer than those of the Arctics and the complete lack of any grey in the plumage left me in no doubt that the bird was a Roseate Tern, probably caught up in the huge movement that was taking place.

Bird of the spring was without doubt the Spotted Crake which took up territory in a large dense patch of irises to the south of Whitehall Village. This bird was discovered by two locals who independently identified it on call and alerted us to it. It could be heard calling from considerable distance and was audible from the pub, the pier, the restaurant, and the post office, its whiplash call echoing around the village. The farmer whose land it

The calling Spotted Crake could be heard echoing around the village

was on immediately offered to remove his cattle from the area to avoid disturbance to the bird – a magnificent gesture and typical of the local farming community – and the bird was present for several weeks subsequently although breeding was not proved. No attempt to see the bird was made other than from long range.

An injured Whimbrel was brought to us in late spring and we soon realised that it would not fly again due to its injuries. As it appeared to be in generally good health we decided to release it on the edge of the moor close to the old Rothiesholm school, ideal breeding habitat for the species, and it is interesting to note that Whimbrel have nested in the area in subsequent years.

"The area around the old school is excellent for migrants"

The area around the old school is excellent for migrants, and Redstarts in particular can often be found in the overgrown playground among the derelict buildings and walls.

Much of our initial planting at the Reserve that year was carried out in late spring and in spite of much care and attention we had got one vital element wrong – it was one of the driest summers on record and a number of small trees died in spite of regular watering. The Reserve soil is extremely sandy and we have since moved some of the remaining trees and shrubs into the garden for protection from the elements. These are now flourishing and have attracted several species of warbler to the garden, and Linnets which had been prospecting for nest-sites in the last few years finally nested in 1995.

The wild-flowers fared rather better, in particular the poppies and corncockle which we had mixed with the oats during sowing. Cornflowers too did well and we discovered wild pansy and orchids close to the house.

The Orkney Farming and Wildlife Advisory Group were most helpful at this time, particularly regarding choice of endemic wild-flower species which would tolerate our soil-type. Many local farms now benefit from similar help and a number have obtained grants for tree planting etc.

By mid-summer the Bu Loch on the Rothiesholm peninsula had completely dried up for the first time in decades and much of the island was suffering from the lack of rain. There appeared to be just two calling Corncrakes left – a decline lamented by visitors and islanders alike – but nesting Pintail were present in good numbers and several broods were seen. Stronsay holds up to a third of the British breeding population of Pintail although like other species of duck they are difficult to monitor. The present number breeding is probably in the region of ten to fifteen pairs, some nesting in wet ditches etc. well away from the lochs. The drakes may fly off to the small offshore islands making any census of the species even more difficult. Two pairs regularly nest close to the Matpow Loch on the edge of St Catherine's Bay and broods can often be observed there from the road. A car here makes an ideal hide, and one of the successful broods we found in 1988 was later filmed for an R.S.P.B educational video.

The Matpow Loch itself is not only in a picturesque setting but is also an important stopping-off point for many species of wader on migration. The edge of the loch is carpeted by a procession of different wild-flowers including marsh marigolds, orchids and ragged robin. A large area of yellow iris and a dense patch of rare sedge make this one of the most attractive sites on the island.

Our 'open day' in late August gave us the opportunity to thank all those who had helped us to set up the Reserve. Many local farms had given us trailer-loads of stone and soil etc., all of which we had put to good use, and a number of bird species had been attracted to the area as a result of this. Our local councillor gave an encouraging speech and 'Radio Orkney' and 'The Orcadian' newspaper were both

The Opening Ceremony

represented at the opening ceremony when our 'Stronsay Bird Reserve' sign was unveiled. Many of those present asked us what the species depicted on the sign was and why we had chosen Yellow-breasted Bunting. It was then that we realised that we may have been over-optimistic and chosen 'a bird too far'. Only time would tell!

We made an interesting ornithological discovery that year whilst sea-watching at Bomasty Bay on the west side of the Rothiesholm peninsula. Although we had seen Sooty Shearwaters to the east of the island over the open sea on many occasions, we were surprised to find a regular flight path of the species through the Stronsay Firth between the North Sea and the Atlantic Ocean.

The Sooty Shearwaters of course have to run the gauntlet among the local skuas and we have occasionally seen individuals knocked into the sea by Great Skuas. What is particularly interesting is that the skuas – which appear to eat almost any other species of bird they can kill – do not eat the Sooty Shearwaters. One can only assume it is the taste!

The loch at Matpow – superb habitat

The loch at Matpow had produced several interesting waders by late August when our attention turned to our oats which were beginning to ripen, and we wondered – "Would our quarter of an acre of oats attract anything but the local sparrows and a handful of Reed Buntings?" We had sown it rather early in the hope that it would ripen before the other few acres on the island and that at least had worked.

Autumn 1989 was not the best we have known on the island for birds. There had been very few waders in early autumn and the lack of easterly winds throughout much of the period meant that many regularly recorded species were either absent or present in below-average numbers. Just one Barred Warbler in the whole period and the only Common Rosefinch was discovered at the far end of the island feeding on dock seeds close to a rocky shore – a far cry from our oats and sandy beach!

Then on the 11th September a small arrival of migrants raised our hopes and we drove round much of the island searching all the likely places for something unusual. By lunch we returned home and almost immediately a small plain-looking bird flitted out of our oats as we drove towards the house. It disappeared into the far side of the crop and we cautiously approached the area, peering over the end of the garden wall and scanning through the ripening oats hardly daring to breathe.

Suddenly a familiar canary-like "whooeeet" attracted our attention and there in the very top of the oats looking straight at us was our very own Common Rosefinch! It was plain and drab – as most of them are – but it was there – in our oats. The planting had been worthwhile.

The bird spent the whole day on the Reserve, even visiting the garden on occasions when it joined the local sparrows drinking at the garden pond. A memorable day.

There was better to come!

Rosefinch – the first of many to be found feeding in the oats on the Reserve

Although generally a 'westerly' autumn – the worst direction for bringing migrants from the continent to the northern isles – there were surprises. A group of four students spent a week with us in late September hoping to find a rare bird or two themselves and although their first day on the island was wet with a strong westerly wind, they braved the elements and set off for a sea-watch at Bomasty Bay. Wet and cold they soon gave up and decided to look in the nearby fields for any migrants that might be there. The first bird to fly up as they stepped into the stubble was not only a 'BB' rarity but a species none of them had ever seen before – a Little Bunting, on their very first morning on the island!

Little Bunting – an unexpected find for four students!

Not quite so obliging was the Quail which 3 of the 4 students saw as it flew across a patch of neaps (turnips) near the island airstrip. The group made several subsequent visits to the area – just about as far away as one can get on Stronsay from the Reserve – in the hope that the fourth member might eventually see it, but sadly with no success. A side of birdwatching we all have to get used to!

Late October saw the first really big influx of autumn migrants and as I went to check our oats on the 29th a Lapland Bunting rose from the stubble – it too had been attracted to the oats, and almost immediately another, smaller bunting flew out and went into the thistles and docks along the drive. It clung to one of the dock stems scolding me with its soft "tick" note, it's bright chestnut cheeks almost glowing in the sunshine – the second Little Bunting of the year, and this time in the oats!

Other birds present during that late 'fall' were 14 Blackcaps, 15 Chiffchaffs and two Wheatears – and it was almost November! Water Rail and Woodcock were new for the reserve as was a Long-eared Owl which roosted in the dense fuchsia hedge which hung over the mill stream from our next-door-neighbours garden. The owl was seen daily for several weeks.

The Long-eared Owl which roosted in the dense fuchsia hedge above the mill-stream for several weeks

Again, as if to emphasise the mild winters often encountered in Orkney, four Chiffchaffs were found feeding together in one of the island ditches on the 9th of December and they appeared to be of three distinct races. Racial identification of the species however can be very difficult and we have recorded a bewildering assortment of 'types' during our fifteen years in the northern isles. A few individuals of the race 'tristis' seen elsewhere in Britain in previous years were first identified and later accepted as Greenish Warblers although in our experience Greenish Warblers have proved very distinct from any of the races of Chiffchaff. Of the five autumn records of Greenish Warbler since we came to the island the identification was confirmed in four by virtue of the fact that they were heard singing!

Arctic Warbler (left) and Greenish Warbler, to show the main structural differences between the species. Chiffchaffs never show such obvious pale wing-bars

Two Chiffchaffs seen in December '89 were typical 'British' types with greenish-olive upperparts, whilst one of the other two appeared to be of the 'Scandinavian' race 'abietinus'. The fourth bird was typical of the 'Siberian' race, being very pale fawny-grey above with a deep browny-buff wash around the ear-coverts. These late autumn 'Siberian' birds in my experience always show completely black legs and bills which contrast markedly with the birds plumage far more than in birds typical of the 'British' race. They also show a distinct whitish 'wing-bar' on the greater coverts and very obvious pale supercilium. A bird showing characters of the 'Siberian' race was present on our turning-circle just outside the house for two days in late autumn 1989. I have also seen birds closely resembling Dusky Warbler in general upperpart tones on both Stronsay and Fair Isle in late autumn (early Dec.). The blackish legs and bills of these birds and generally 'clean' under-parts confirmed their identification as Chiffchaffs but given brief views it would be easy to initially misidentify such birds.

Sadly many of the late autumn migrants fall prey to Merlins and as I watched the four Chiffchaffs feeding in the ditch in December that year, a male Merlin appeared to be eyeing the quartet from the top of the nearby drying-kiln.

"A male Merlin appeared to be eyeing the quartet from the top of the nearby drying-kiln"

The sheltered yard at Holland Farm

1990

1990 began with a 'bang' against the window and a flurry of feathers as a Merlin caught one of our wintering Skylarks and carried it off to the roof of one of our out-buildings where it was plucked and eaten. There seems no doubt that Skylarks are a favourite prey of Merlins in winter and during our time both here and on Fair Isle many have fallen to this dashing little falcon.

The days have begun to lengthen noticeably by early February and some species such as Oystercatcher and Stonechat begin to move north during the month.

The Great Skuas begin to arrive back on their nesting grounds by March and as they fly across the island in their peculiarly sinister lop-sided manner cause absolute havoc among the bird population. All birds are petrified of Great Skuas which is not surprising as I have seen many sudden horrific attacks by them on a wide range of species, including gulls, waders, ducks including

Eider and even a fully grown Mute Swan cygnet! The latter only managed to escape the skuas aerial lunges by swaying its neck out of range each time the skua attacked, while the parent swans looked on helpless from nearby. After a few minutes of persistent aerial attacks the skua finally gave up and flew off.

The local breeding Arctic Skuas return towards the end of April and occasionally 'get it wrong', arriving back on the island before the Arctic Terns which they parasitise for food. When this occurs the skuas are forced to look for food elsewhere and can often be seen chasing waders and other species over the island lochs. Once the bulk of the terns arrive – usually in early May – the skuas return to their preferred routine and from then on can be seen harassing terns for food throughout the summer. In view of this it is hard to understand why the largest regular colony of breeding Arctic Terns on Stronsay is situated virtually alongside the colonies of Arctic and Great Skuas!

There were several additions to the island list in 1990 – a Grasshopper Warbler "reeling" at the Reserve; a Bean Goose flying over the Reserve after being seen at the Matpow Loch earlier; a

A first-summer Hobby on a road-side fence-post

Hobby which was present for over a week in early June, and a brilliant red adult male Crossbill picked up wet and bedraggled in our drive late one evening. The Crossbill was the first of what turned out to be a huge invasion into the U.K. from the continent.

Male Crossbill – the first of a huge invasion

Flocks could be seen all over the island during the summer, feeding mainly on thistle-heads along the sides of the roads. One flock numbered 250 and as they rose from the thistles on the dunes at Rothiesholm I noticed one slightly smaller bird . The alarm-bells rang immediately! Surely this must be a Two-barred Crossbill!

Amazingly, in spite of much searching I could not relocate the flock which had gone out of sight behind the farm at the 'Bu'.

Although there are comparatively few birders out looking for passerine migrants in mid-summer it can be a productive time, particularly during hot spells of weather with light SE winds. During our time on Fair Isle we had noticed how species such as Red-backed Shrike and Marsh Warbler would turn up in these weather conditions. Honey Buzzard too is a species that is likely to appear in mid-summer.

One such spell occurred in July 1990 when a Marsh Warbler appeared in the mill stream ditch next to the reserve, ironically just as we set off for the 'plane with departing visitors. On our return to 'Castle' we were immediately alerted to a superb adult

Adult Rose-coloured Starling – finally located around the farm buildings at Dale

Rose-coloured Starling at nearby 'Dale' where one had been seen following the silage-cutter. This too was a new bird for Stronsay but it led us a chase until we finally caught up with it around the farm buildings.

The next 'new' bird for the island was also an 'exotic' – Ruddy Shelduck, although there is always the possibility that birds of this species are either escapes from captivity or originate from the small feral breeding population on the continent. The Stronsay

Ruddy Shelduck – perhaps a genuine wild vagrant

bird was extremely wary as I watched it wading in the shallow Bu Loch, and although much has been written on whether or not any recent records of this species refer to genuine wild birds, most writers seem to have missed what may be the main factor governing the occurrence of this species in the U.K. – i.e. the weather conditions in Southern Europe during the breeding season.

The large influx of Ruddy Shelducks into NW Europe in 1892 is well documented and often referred to, and appears to have been as a result of drought conditions in Southern Europe. (This important point was mentioned by Thorburn earlier this century but seems to have been missed by recent writers including 'The Handbook'). Although the breeding range of the species has contracted this century it is possible that at least some of those recorded recently in NW Europe are genuine vagrants. The Stronsay bird was seen to fly into the island high from the east, was present for less than an hour and was not seen again anywhere else in Orkney. A very puzzling species, but it is interesting that on the same day as the Stronsay bird a party of five were seen flying over London – several hundred miles to the south!

Our first Marsh Harrier flew past the Reserve on the 10th August after being located earlier that day near the pond at 'Dale'. It was a young 'chocolate-brown' bird and was later seen hunting around the Meikle Water.

Almost on cue the first influx of small migrants occurred on the 16th August and another huge wave of Crossbills arrived a few days later when hundreds were present on the island. We had several brought in to us exhausted and hungry and it is most pleasing to be able to say that most were released back into the wild after being fed on thistle-heads. Many young birds however did not seem to recognise these as a food-source and we frantically searched for suitable alternatives. Finally we found the answer – porridge oats, which the birds ate with relish giving rise to the question – "Were these Scottish Crossbills?"!

The 1st September brought a third new bird of prey for the island that year – a Honey Buzzard, which drifted slowly south over us as we stood watching the strange behaviour of a party of Swallows and Swifts above the small quarry at 'Gorie's'. They had obviously seen the bird long before we did and began drifting higher above us as the raptor approached, losing all interest in the insects they had been hawking over the water there.

*A Leach's Petrel fighting against the storm above the garage roof
in the hurricane of September 1990*

Probably the most dramatic event of autumn 1990 was the sudden hurricane of September the 19th. The mean wind-speed exceeded 90mph for several hours with gusts well over 100mph. These early storms have a dramatic effect on the landscape, stripping the leaves off all but the most sheltered trees and bushes and turning much of the grazing land from green to brown in just a few hours. Such wind-speeds test the resolve of many who move up to Orkney from further south, but for birdwatchers in particular they are very exciting.

We spent much of the day outside, sea-watching from the car in the lee of our out-buildings and were rewarded with the spectacle of several Leach's and Storm Petrels flying right over the house, desperately fighting against the storm. They had all been swept right across the island before the hurricane-force winds. The Leach's Petrels fared slightly better than their less robust relatives and even held their own for a while under the shore close to where we sat, but they too were eventually driven out of Mill Bay to the east. An adult Long-tailed Skua suffered the same fate as it too flew right over our heads, and an afternoon drive around the island – by which time the mean wind-speed had dropped to around 80mph, revealed more petrels flying into the wind but being gradually driven backwards and out of sight.

By evening the whole island had changed colour and the sea too was an angry shade of brown. The fuchsia hedges had been stripped bare – a big disappointment for ourselves as it meant that there was now very little cover on the island for late migrants which might normally be attracted to the cover of the gardens.

Next day brought more surprises. A Great Spotted Woodpecker was discovered in one of the gardens at Whitehall Village where we found it frantically searching for food on a washing-line post, almost oblivious of our presence. These poor birds really do look out of place on the island and can often be seen working their way along lines of fence-posts.

Great Spotted Woodpecker on a washing-line post in Whitehall Village

Later that day one flew across the Reserve garden and landed with a 'smack' on the old wooden cart we had left in the shore-side field hoping that one day it might attract this very species!

October too opened with a 'bang' when we discovered an Olive-backed Pipit feeding in the tufty grass on the turning circle. This bird, like several others I have seen on Stronsay and Fair Isle seemed to prefer this type of habitat, particularly in the vicinity of low and broken walls.

The 3rd October was one of those 'once-in-a-life-time' never to be forgotten 'red-letter' days.

We received a call from a farmer at 'Cleat' to say that he had seen a strange bird fly up from just outside his garden and land in the nearby ditch. As I set off in the car several species ran through my mind, but I was not prepared for what was to follow! As I arrived the farmer was waiting to greet me and pointed to where the bird had landed. I slowly approached the ditch when suddenly from almost under my feet out flew one of the gems of British ornithology – a superb White's Thrush.

One of the gems of British Ornithology – White's Thrush, the first record for Orkney

The cliffs at Odiness Bay in a spectacular SE storm.
Migrants often arrive in such conditions!

It almost flew into the farmer as it landed back where he had originally seen it, and fortunately its next stop was the nearby garden where it settled down for the rest of the day, giving amazing views as it fed below the fuchsia hedge, often 'bouncing' in the manner of a Jack Snipe.

Many islanders saw it that day, but typical of the species it had gone the following morning and in spite of 2 hours of diligent searching by ourselves and the farmer, the thirty or so keen birders already waiting at John o' Groats at first light were doomed to disappointment.

One interesting point about this bird's arrival was that it appeared to have arrived in the middle of a low pressure system and when found, the wind was NW – exactly the opposite of what is considered to be the best direction for the arrival of such species. The Fair Isle Red-flanked Bluetail of 1981 also arrived in similar circumstances.

In mid-October that year a newly-fledged Storm Petrel was found in a small walled yard next to Kelp Stores in Whitehall Village.

The newly-fledged Storm Petrel prior to its release into Mill Bay.
Some downy feathers can be seen on the nape

It was brought to us and appeared unharmed – it had probably just 'got it wrong' on its first flight.

After some deliberation we decided to feed it on the oil from tinned sardines and then to let it go in Mill Bay. There was a strong SW wind blowing and so we took the bird close to the shore where it was sheltered, but twice on release there the bird just fluttered down helpless onto the sand. There seemed just one last hope and so we decided to take the bird up above the beach and launch it into the almost gale-force wind. Unbeknown to us this appeared to be just what the bird wanted and as I pointed it into the wind and let go, it gave a couple of gleeful flicks of its wings and flew straight out to sea, dancing across the waves as it went.

More excellent species were found that autumn including Barred Warblers, Red-breasted Flycatcher and our third island Little Bunting, and during a big influx of Goldcrests on the 24th October a Pallas's Warbler was found feeding among the short turf near Lamb Head. As with many of those seen during the big influx on Fair Isle in 1982 this bird seemed to prefer short turf close to the cliffs and fed very much in the manner of the Goldcrests which also seem to prefer this habitat.

Back on the Reserve a Jack Snipe took up residence in our potato patch and was seen on several occasions towards the end of the year, whilst our small herd of cattle were now inside for the winter.

We had come to appreciate the value of a small grazing herd for creating a different type of habitat and we now often tether one of the older cows in a particular area we need to be grazed outside the normal grassy fields. This also prevents the whole area becoming overgrown with weeds, something we are keen to avoid, although certain areas on the Reserve are allowed to revert to wildflower margins.

Each year it has been brought home to us that birds may turn up just about anywhere on the island and old farm machinery in particular often attracts migrants.

Birds may turn up just about anywhere on the island

We alerted other local birdwatchers to the Dotterel
from the old red telephone-box nearby

1991

There was a very puzzling occurrence on the 1st January 1991.
One of the farmers at 'Rosebank' in the NW corner of the island had found a Little Auk stranded in the middle of a field and brought it to us. The wind at the time was light, and after feeding the bird on tinned sardines we released it into the almost still waters of Mill Bay right outside the house. The bird swam a few yards out to sea, dived, began washing and preening and to our amazement almost immediately a second Little Auk took off from the water several hundred yards away and flew right over the bird we had just released.

How this second bird had located the first is a complete mystery and ornithologists have recently been asking this question, particularly regarding rare breeding species, when a mate has turned up at a site several days after the first bird has set up territory. The answer may be quite simple with common species where natural abundance may be a big factor but may not be so with rarities. Whether it is sight, sound or a combination of these and other factors which enables birds to locate each other from considerable distance remains one of ornithology's unsolved mysteries.

We decided to sow a second area of oats in 1991 and this was rewarded in the autumn when several Common Rosefinches visited the Reserve, including two together for almost a week!

The installation of a small garden pond also paid dividends as the Rosefinches used this regularly for drinking and bathing and they could be seen from the comfort of the sitting-room and the kitchen. This was a new species for many of our visitors and we could celebrate instantly with a cup of tea or coffee!

Mid-April sees a mass exodus of the wintering species from Stronsay and on still clear evenings flocks of Curlew in particular can be seen flying off north-east towards Shetland. Most of the several thousand Golden Plover which winter here have left by this time and we begin to look forward to more unexpected species taking their place.

A car arrived amidst a cloud of dust on the evening of 22nd April to alert us to a Snowy Owl which had been discovered near Kirbister. It turned out to be an almost pure white adult male and we alerted as many people as possible before dark. It was enjoyed by a whole host that evening but in spite of much searching could not be relocated next day.

Snowy Owl – sadly only present for one evening

Both Glaucous and Iceland Gulls were present on the island well into May by which time they were to be found feeding on freshly ploughed fields in company with other gulls. The first-summer Glaucous Gull was last seen on the Blan Loch towards the end of the month.

The pair of Dotterel found on the edge of the Rothiesholm moor close to the old school on May 28th were very obliging and we alerted other observers to them from the old red 'phone-box there. These birds were more considerate than the owl and in spite of flying off that evening were relocated next day almost five miles away at 'Airy'. As usual they were very tame, allowing close approach and stunning views.

There was yet another intriguing sighting on the 12th June 1991. A party of 9 'greater' Snow Geese were located flying north-east across the island by one of our visitors as we searched for late spring migrants. The party flew right over us and headed off out to sea in the direction of Shetland giving us cause to consider that they may have been genuine migrants heading for the breeding

A Glaucous Gull (foreground) with other gulls at the Blan Loch near Mt. Pleasant in May

grounds in Greenland. All were 'white phase' adults and as there had been several days of strong westerly winds across the North Atlantic prior to their discovery it seems quite feasible that these were genuine wild birds attempting to reach the breeding grounds.

We were alerted to yet another 'white' bird a day or so later and it turned out to be an albino juvenile House Sparrow.

Yet another 'white' bird – this time an albino House Sparrow

July 11th was hot with a light SE wind and 'felt' good for birds and at 8.45am we received an urgent call from our next-door-neighbour – the island nurse – to say that she had seen a very exotic 'parrot-like' bird with yellow in its plumage fly out of the nearby over-grown garden. Expecting the bird to be a Golden Oriole we dashed across to search the dense fuchsia bushes in the hope of locating it, but after ten minutes had drawn a complete blank. We returned at lunchtime armed with photographs and field-guides in the hope that our neighbour would be able to identify the bird from them. There was no need, for as we arrived there, a beautiful Bee-eater flew out of the garden and right over our heads to the delight of ourselves and our neighbours.

*Our next-door-neighbour found this beautiful Bee-eater
in a nearby garden on a hot day in July*

The bird spent the whole day hawking over the fields around the Reserve and many islanders came to see it.

There was a funny incident during that hot spell when a family who had just moved into the island spotted a small sailing-boat coming ashore just below their house 'Lower Dishes'. They went to see if they could give help in any way and asked the crew how far they had come. "From Holland" came the reply, which caused great consternation among the family who were concerned for the crew's safety. Some considerable time after the yacht had set out to sea again the family were to discover that 'Holland' is in fact a farm just two miles from where the boat had come ashore!!

What was surely a Booted Warbler was found in a dense fuchsia garden in late August

The most puzzling bird of the year however was found in a dense fuchsia garden on 23rd of August. It was present for three days but for a number of reasons (mainly lack of time!) I only managed to obtain fleeting views except when photographing it on the 25th. This gave rise to a problem with the identification and stands as a cautionary tale to all who use photographs to prove the identification of some difficult species. The initial set of photographs, although clear, had not been printed true to colour – although I did not realise this at the time – giving the bird a slightly greenish hue, and for over two years I 'shelved' the bird.

In 1994 I decided to obtain a second set of prints and these now showed a totally different picture. The bird now appeared 'browner'

A Long-tailed Skua flying past the attractive sandstone house at Mount Pleasant

and confirmed my suspicions that it was almost certainly a Booted Warbler.

It is amazing how often 'first impressions' are correct and how we can be swayed by what appears to be photographic evidence.

Grey Phalarope was new for the island on the 5th September and there were many sightings of porpoises during what is often the best month for cetaceans. An amazingly confiding adult Long-tailed Skua was found feeding on a dead rabbit in the middle of the road near Mt. Pleasant on the 12th and I decided to move the corpse to the grass verge as the bird was in danger of being run down by passing vehicles. I was barely six feet away from the

*An amazingly confiding Long-tailed Skua was found feeding
on a dead rabbit near Mount Pleasant*

corpse when the skua returned and commenced feeding.

It is uncanny how many of our Long-tailed Skua records are from this part of the island. Nearly all have been adults, and many of these have been seen flying over near the attractive sandstone house at Mt. Pleasant.

At least 3 Common Rosefinches were found on the Reserve in September often visiting the garden pond to drink and bathe. A brilliant male Bluethroat was found in the sub-post office garden on the 6th October. Partly hidden by the wall there, four of our visitors and ourselves waited patiently, hoping that it would appear in the open. We were soon rewarded when it ran straight towards us and began feeding just a few feet from where we stood.

A big arrival of Song Thrushes occurred on the 8th when small parties could be seen in many places. A strange sight when one considers that the species is generally regarded as solitary!

Unexpected sightings are always the most memorable, none more so than the one at The Pow on the 9th October. I had taken two visitors to the area to look for Purple Sandpipers which winter there in good numbers and as we scanned the foreshore we noticed a smallish black bill with a yellow tip protruding from behind a rock. Almost immediately the bird walked out into full view and our suspicions were confirmed – it was an adult Sabine's Gull – our first American species of gull for the island! We watched it preening and briefly in flight for a few minutes but it soon departed to the east. It had been pure good fortune that we had chosen that time to visit the area in what had been a quick run out before dinner!

There was a big influx of continental migrants about this time including many Bramblings, and a Red-breasted Flycatcher was seen, but totally unexpected was the number of Ring Ouzels present on the island. Nine were seen together in our next-door-neighbours garden and two took up residence on our front lawn. Quite astounding as the species is generally so wary.

At such times it is often possible to see birds arriving on the island during day-light hours. These periods of visual migration are very exciting for birdwatchers. Calling thrushes, mere dots when first detected can be seen dropping almost vertically from the sky.

Rosefinch – this one like many others joined up with the local sparrow flock

These newly-arrived birds often announce their presence both vocally and by their alert agitated behaviour.

Many of our visitors come to the island in the hope of finding their own rare birds, and such a couple in 1991 had set their sights on Richard's Pipit, a species they had never seen previously in the U.K. Sadly they did not find one during their stay but what they did find was even rarer and yet in the same family – an Olive-backed Pipit! This bird was again feeding in long tufty grass close to a low wall, and as we all returned home to celebrate we almost ran over a second bird as it fed along the entrance to our drive. A quite amazing ten minutes, and again we enjoyed close-up views from the car without disturbing the bird.

A Tree Pipit on October 29th reminded us that this species too can appear very late in the northern isles.

Olive-backed Pipit – an unexpected bonus for our visitors

The old derelict Manse and overgrown garden

1992

Because so few small passerines winter on the island it is usually easy to detect migration on Stronsay in early spring. Pied Wagtails, noticeable by their absence in winter, return in early March and good numbers of other nesting species such as Meadow pipits and Linnets arrive some time later. Similarly, with so few small nesting species here – no Robins, Dunnocks or Greenfinches for example – these too can be confidently identified as migrants.

Wheatears are only occasionally seen here before April, and the bigger 'Greenland' birds are generally passing north through Orkney in the middle of May. There was a big influx of the latter 'sub-species' in mid-May '92 when hundreds were present on the 17th, but in the clear skies and light winds all had moved on by the following morning – an amazing exodus.

Having already found a singing male Bluethroat on the 23rd and a female on the 24th May, we were already well into the season for exotic species that year and totally unprepared for the most astonishing arrival of a single species I have ever witnessed. Suddenly on the 27th there were Spotted Flycatchers everywhere and we could see at least twenty from the house alone. By evening we had counted no less than 500 and this was probably a gross underestimate as we only covered part of the island. Every garden had at least three and every farm at least a dozen around the buildings. The previous highest day total in spring for the island was less than 10!

Several Wood Warblers arrived at the same time but unlike the flycatchers these looked completely lost and many were giving a plaintive distress call. One even attempted to get into the 'byre' through one of the 'arrow-slits' in its desperate search for food.

Excellent numbers of exciting species were seen at the end of the month including no less than 7 Icterine Warblers, 6 Common Rosefinches – including one red singing male – 3 female Bluethroats and an amazing 22 Red-backed Shrikes! One brief car-drive to post a few letters on the evening of May 30th revealed 4

One of the 'arrow-slit' windows in the 'byre'

Icterines, Bluethroat, Common Rosefinch and Red-backed Shrike – all seen without leaving the vehicle!

The warm spell in June brought no less than three Marsh Warblers to the island – 2 of them singing, and a Quail could be heard calling at 'Dale' where the bird of the spring was seen on the 6th June – a Nightjar. It was discovered by the farmer and his wife who had gone out just before midnight to check their cattle, and had suddenly become aware of the bird catching moths in the headlights of their car.

There was yet another new species for the island during the late spring when two drake Mandarins were found by farmers ploughing close to the small loch at Hescombe.

The Bu Loch was next to provide us with a new species for the island since we arrived in 1987, when on the 29th June an adult female Red-necked Phalarope was found 'spinning' as it fed in the shallow water. There are one or two fairly recent records for the island and the species has certainly bred on Stronsay this century, probably around the Meikle Water loch where the vegetation in places looks ideal for nesting. This bird proved very popular among the islanders and a whole procession of cars came along to see it. Its popularity certainly had something to do with the fact that the species is so tame and it was therefore easy to locate and watch!

As we drove towards the loch on the 4th July in the hope of another look at the phalarope we became aware of a bird flying away from us along the road some way ahead. It looked 'suspicious' and I pulled in to look for it as it appeared to have landed on a fence close to the road. We were looking directly into the sun but as we had suspected, there on the top wire next to the road was our second island adult Rose-coloured Starling! Sue had managed to miss the first one in 1990 and we thought her chance had gone – after all, none had been recorded on Fair Isle during our six years there! This bird like the previous one fed among the freshly-cut silage, generally among the huge flock of common Starlings when it could be difficult to locate, but fortunately it was very predictable during the early evenings when it would visit the partly renovated house 'St Catherine's' for half an hour or so to preen and rest. Again many people came to see the bird but it was very wary and certainly did not appear to be a candidate for the 'escape' category.

4 returning Icterine Warblers were seen on 9th August – a record autumn day total – and we watched a Wryneck being pursued in flight by a Meadow Pipit on the 24th, behaviour we have noted in the Northern Isles a few times. It seems as if other small birds cannot quite make out just what Wrynecks are and although they do not exactly 'mob' them will follow them, both on the ground and in flight. I have located several Wrynecks by observing the behaviour of other small species nearby.

*Two drake Mandarins were discovered by a farmer
ploughing near the loch at Hescombe*

More migrants on the 26th included our 5th island Greenish
Warbler, and amazingly it was discovered in the same small
sycamore as one of the birds of 1988. It too sang regularly – even in
heavy drizzle – as had three of the previous four.

Classic 'fall' conditions occurred overnight on 30th–31st August
1992. From 4pm on the 30th the wind strengthened from the SE and
by midnight was between gale force 8 to storm 10 with heavy rain.
By first light on the 31st it was calm and there had been another
huge influx of mainly woodland species including good numbers of
Garden Warblers, Pied Flycatchers and Willow Warblers. 2
Ortolans were found – one at the Kirk, and the other, in a strange
almost eerie parallel, nearly two miles away at the graveyard! The

Ortolan Bunting on the Kirk wall

80

two birds were quite different, one showing a greenish wash to the head whereas the other appeared to be a typical autumn juvenile with huge 'sub-moustachial' stripes. The bird near the Kirk was found feeding in the road outside and when finally disturbed by a passing motorist flew up onto the small wall surrounding the Kirk grounds where it gave even better views.

The 21st of September 1992 will to us always be The Day! As I stepped out of the house that morning it <u>felt</u> good for birds! A light SE wind and very 'muggy'. A group of birdwatchers bound for Fair Isle had been stuck on the island over the week-end due to fog and all were lamenting the fact that one of the species they really hoped to see during their holiday there was Yellow-breasted Bunting, and that the one which had been present on Fair Isle over

The ultimate prize – a Yellow-breasted Bunting in our oats!

the week-end had disappeared. Finding themselves a Barred Warbler during their brief stay on Stronsay hardly compensated for the bunting!

My third visit to the oats at 11am on Monday 21st revealed one of the small local Reed Bunting flock calling down from a low fence-wire to a bird feeding on the ground below. I could barely make out the shape of the bird on the ground until it suddenly hopped out into the open, and there among the very oats we had sown for it was our own Yellow-breasted Bunting. Our optimism had after all been justified – our 'logo' had come to life!

I dashed indoors to alert the group and within ten minutes they had arrived in borrowed car and taxi. All we had to do then was to relocate the bird – the group had just over an hour before their 'plane was due to leave for Fair Isle.

A frustrating ten minutes was spent searching the area and after our third lap of the oats we decided to spread out.

A shout went up from the group searching close to the shore and I could tell by their expressions that they had located the bunting. I edged slowly across towards them by which time the telescopes were focussed on it as it fed among the weeds close to the turning circle.

The expressions said it all – the Yellow-breasted Bunting had been found!

After a few minutes the bird flew up, went right across the front garden and settled back in the oats where I had first located it earlier that morning. Once again the 'scopes were focussed on the bird, but this time from the back yard where we all watched it feeding in the oats whilst we enjoyed a celebratory coffee. It was a new bird for all but one of the group of seven bound for Fair Isle, and for ourselves the ultimate achievement – we had done it!!!

Although rather 'drab' for the species, it is interesting to note that our bird's description matched that of the one that was last seen

The happy group who saw the Yellow-breasted Bunting
just before they left for Fair Isle

on Fair Isle the previous day, and it seems quite probable that they were one and the same.

The next big arrival of birds occurred on October 1st when a female 'eastern' Stonechat was found.

This proved to be an exciting spell and our first island Red-throated Pipit flew up from almost under our feet as we went to check the garden at 'Fingeo' on the 2nd. Unfortunately this bird – like so many of the species in the UK – could not be relocated and was identified mainly on call.

The 3rd was even better with Great Grey Shrike and another 'eastern' Stonechat – this time a male – found by one of our visitors as it fed along the shore next to the Reserve. Bird of the day however, was the immaculate Rustic Bunting which was discovered from the kitchen window as we were about to set off to the shop. It was perched on top of the branch we had stuck in the ground there in the hope that one day it might produce a rare bird for us. It had – and what a bird! It was seen later that day on the turning-circle and in the vegetable garden.

The second 'eastern' Stonechat of the autumn was a beautiful male at the Reserve

This was the third rare bunting we had recorded feeding on the turning-circle weeds (following the Yellow-breasted and Little Buntings) and proved the value of even quite small areas of this type of habitat. The mixture of endemic weeds, wild flowers and oats is obviously a great attraction to seed-eaters and the same turning-circle has now hosted at least a dozen Rosefinches and an Arctic Redpoll.

At this time of year the roadside ditches really come into their own. Much of the vegetation has by now died back and birds can be seen quite easily as they work their way along in the shelter the ditches afford.

As I approached one such ditch close to our daughter's house at

The immaculate Rustic Bunting first seen from the kitchen window

At this time of the year the roadside ditches really come into their own.
This one held Sardinian Warbler in late October 1992

Airy Cottage on the 29th October 1992, a small bird flitted along
the centre of the ditch and out of sight. As I rounded the bend,
there, on top of the dry-stone wall, was an adult male Sardinian
Warbler.

Although I had never seen the species before there was no doubt,
and although it could be elusive on occasions, we were to enjoy
tremendous views of it over the next two days when the red eye and
eye-ring could be clearly seen.

This was probably the most unexpected discovery since we came
to the island and a great end to the autumn migration. There
appeared to be very few migrants on the island at the time but as
is often the case in the northern isles extreme rarities often turn

"There, on top of the dry-stone wall, was an adult male Sardinian Warbler"

Sardinian Warbler – found in a roadside ditch!

up when there are very few other migrants present. This was the case with the White's Thrush of October 1990 and the Red-flanked Bluetail on Fair Isle in September 1981, but the phenomenon is in fact more noticeable in late spring when half the passerine migrants present will often be rarities or semi-rarities. In late May and early June the commonest migrants can be Red-backed Shrikes, Rosefinches, Icterine Warblers or Marsh Warblers and of course this is the prime time for the super-rarities for which Orkney and Shetland are well-known.

It can be a very frustrating time too as migrants in late spring often move on very rapidly after a short rest, and I remember an old Fair-Islander shaking his head as a group of birders there rushed off to look for a late spring Rustic Bunting. "They'll not see that again," he smiled – and they didn't!

Although it is not wise to generalise, in spring it is as well to enjoy the moment.

The autumn generally affords more prolonged opportunities for studying migrants in the northern isles and in favourable conditions many birds will stay faithful to the same area for days or even weeks. Some species however are notorious 'one-day' stayers – rare thrushes for example – as many birdwatchers have learnt to their cost!

Clear skies at night and a cold NW wind is the worst possible combination in autumn and many migrants depart in such conditions.

Migrants are generally more obliging in the autumn.
The Arctic Redpoll of November 1988 spent several days in the Reserve garden

Old Mill Wheel on the Reserve

1993

The Stonechats which arrived on the Reserve in late 1992 were present until a cold spell of weather in February '93. Chiffchaff and Woodcock were also seen on the Reserve during January and a Glaucous Gull on 28th February.

The sludgy ditch-cleanings imported in late '92 were used to create mounds either side of the drive which were later sown with a mixture of wild-flower seeds by a group of children from the local school. By mid-summer we had the most fantastic display of poppies, cornflowers, corncockle and corn marigolds. Many on the island visited the Reserve just to see the wonderful display of colours and several farms were later given some of the seed from them for sowing on their own land.

SE winds in early April brought good numbers of migrants to us including Ring Ouzel and Black Redstart, the latter taking up residence on our midden (dung-heap!) for several days. 800

Fieldfares were seen on the 11th and an island rarity – Wood Pigeon was seen on the 14th. A Great Grey Shrike spent the day around the Reserve on the 24th by which time the local Skylarks and Meadow Pipits were in full song and nest-building.

Two of our first guests that year had come to Stronsay hoping to find a male Bluethroat, and although early May was exceptionally cold, easterly winds again did the trick. As we approached one of the species' favourite ditches we could hear the Bluethroat singing

Typical view of a spring male Bluethroat – singing in a ditch!

before we saw it, and incredibly, as we were watching it, an Icterine Warbler flew up onto the flagstone alongside. Both species were new birds for our visitors who made several subsequent visits to the area during their holiday!

As we were watching the Bluethroat an Icterine Warbler flew up onto the flagstone alongside

A more typical view of an Icterine Warbler in one of the island gardens

By the 15th the same ditch held no less than 3 Bluethroats – 2 of which were singing males – Redstart, Lesser Whitethroat, Sedge Warbler, the Icterine Warbler and a Tree pipit!

No further male Bluethroats were seen in spring that year but there were sightings of several females up until the 23rd. 2 beautiful summer-plumaged Slavonian Grebes were seen in late May, one of which was found close to the main pier at Whitehall village. A 'brown' Common Rosefinch was found in the escallonia hedge at the sub post-office at the end of the month and it too was first seen by one of our visitors who had come to Stronsay in the hope of finding such a species.

Early June was rather cool and migration came to a virtual halt. As a result of this, a couple who were staying with us decided to concentrate their efforts on filming seals.

Finding a secluded stretch of rocky coast-line they began filming and were delighted when a family party of Shelducks swam into view just beyond the seals. Continuing to film they hardly noticed a party of four waders fly in and land 'in the frame', but suddenly realising that three were obviously adult Dunlin and the other was considerably smaller, they turned their attention to these, and in particular the smallest bird.

An hour or so later they arrived back at the house and showed the film to ourselves and our other visitor. The smallest wader looked interesting to say the least and we had a hasty tea and returned to the site in the hope of relocating it.

It did not take the group of us long to find it and over the next two hours we took copious notes and made several field-sketches.

We had decided from the film that there were only three realistic possibilities – Little Stint, Western Sandpiper and Semi-palmated Sandpiper, and almost as soon as we arrived Little Stint was eliminated on call alone as the bird was heard to call on 2 or 3 occasions. (It was heard several times that evening and again the following day.) The call itself was a very dry "drrrrt", very low and 'flat' sounding, quite different from the higher-pitched "chit" of Little Stint.

We knew that Separating Western Sandpiper from Semi-palmated Sandpiper can be very difficult, but as is often the case with small American waders in the U.K., our bird was very approachable and as a result we were able to study it very closely for long periods. On top of that, because of the latitude we were able to watch it in good light until 10pm at which time we returned to the reserve to study the literature.

It did not take us long to decide, and independently we all came to the conclusion that our bird was a Semi-palmated Sandpiper – only the second ever recorded in Scotland.

The following day we all returned to the site, and finding the bird still in the same area we obtained further excellent views. There was no doubt that it was a Semi-palmated Sandpiper and eventually the couple who originally found the bird saw the palmations between the toes when the bird perched on a pale dry rock just a few yards from them. This immediately ruled out all but Western Sandpiper which was eliminated on bill-length and lack of rufous in the plumage other than on the cheeks and sides of the crown.

Another great rarity for the island.

Semi-palmated Sandpiper – yet another 'first for Orkney'
and only the second ever in Scotland

1993 was without doubt, our most colourful year at the Reserve. Not only were the mounds in the drive a real picture but the oats, which had been admixed with wild-flower seed when sown were the best they have ever looked. These areas of cultivation were the most beautiful soft mixture of pink, blue and yellows which contrasted perfectly with the ripening oats. (see page 112.)

There was an excellent late-summer passage of common waders that year and a juvenile Red-necked Phalarope was found 'spinning' in the small pond next to the island water-pumping station near Whitehall Village. Our first island male Marsh Harrier was discovered hunting around the marshy perimeter of the Meikle Water where it could be seen from the Reserve, and another lost-looking adult Long-tailed Skua drifted over the island in early September.

The big 'fall' on the 11th September brought no less than 25 Redstarts to the island and a Wryneck was watched feeding in the drive after flying from one of the mounds of wild-flowers.

A Wryneck was found in the Reserve drive

A Bluethroat was found just a few yards from another Wryneck on the 13th and when visiting the site to look for the Wryneck on the 20th, we found that its companion was not the Bluethroat but our second island Yellow-breasted Bunting!

Although most 'rare' migrants which turn up on the island are found in the 'wrong' habitat, one bird of late autumn '93 at 'Airy' got it right, and it too was a new species for Orkney.

Our son-in-law's farm had recently extended their slurry-pit which now looked very much like a miniature working quarry, and as I passed it on the 27th September an unfamiliar loud call greeted me. There, among the tyre-marks in the bottom of the pit was a Little Ringed Plover, but how it had found the almost ideal habitat is a mystery and particularly so when one considers that it was the first record of the species for Orkney.

Little-Ringed Plover – new for Orkney, and this time in suitable habitat!

93

We decided to create a new, much larger pond that autumn and positioned it opposite the turning circle where there was still a good show of wild flowers. One of the first birds seen drinking from it was yet another Common Rosefinch and a party of 3 Goldfinches was also attracted to the 40ft x 6ft stretch of water. Sadly, the remains of one of these was later found on the edge of the pond, yet another lost migrant which has fallen prey to a Merlin.

Wild flowers on the turning-circle in late autumn

A number of endemic water-plants were added to the pond in our efforts to create a natural-looking environment.

October started where September finished off, with more rare and interesting species. These included Olive-backed Pipit, Richard's Pipit and Red-breasted flycatcher, and many other species were seen including Grasshopper Warbler.

The 10th October started well with a Richard's Pipit strutting around our oats which we had recently flattened as an experiment. We hoped that by covering up some of the seed this could be exposed by ourselves as the autumn progressed, thereby providing food for any birds which may be present later in the year. Severe autumn gales normally flatten any standing crops and so this year we decided to do it first! We were later to discover that our idea was a great success.

The Richard's Pipit certainly seemed to enjoy this newly created habitat and it was seen there several times over the next couple of days.

Fired with enthusiasm after finding the Richard's Pipit, I set off with our last visitor of the year to look for more migrants.

As we walked alongside one of the ditches near Lamb Head a small dark 'phylloscopus' warbler flew out of the undergrowth and scolded us with its hard "tack" note. We ducked down quickly behind the flagstone wall and looked at each other in amazement. There was just this one bird in the ditch and yet there could be no doubt about the identification – it was a Dusky Warbler!

It was extremely vocal, calling at the slightest disturbance, the "tack" call on occasions running into a staccato-like trill, but it was not easy to observe, diving into deep cover along the edge of the ditch at every opportunity.

Only the third ever to be seen in Orkney and yet it was not even a new bird for Stronsay! The first British record of this species was discovered on the off – shore island of Auskerry, less than three miles from where we were standing, on the 1st of October 1913. We could clearly see the lighthouse there, and our minds went back to those pioneers of British ornithology earlier this century who realised the potential of the northern isles for study-ing migration.

Quite by chance a large pipit was discovered feeding in the small area of grass between the road and the sub post-office on the 24th October. The initial views of the bird from the car at very close range – less than fifteen yards – suggested a large Tree Pipit but it was obviously too big for that species. It had a very horizontal stance but in general colouration and structure closely resembled a typical Richard's Pipit.

What was most puzzling was the fact that the bird was so tame and even when approached closely flew only a short distance. The call was a rather quiet "bjeeoow chup chup" – quite unlike the normal strident "reeeiip" of Richard's Pipit.

Dusky Warbler – just three miles from the site of the first British record in October 1913

The wing-coverts were all unmoulted juvenile feathers which did not help with the identification but the call and tameness strongly suggest Blyth's Pipit – another major rarity.

A late Bluethroat and a Ring Ouzel were seen on the 29th and our first island Woodlark was found in a stubble-field packed with Twite, Skylarks and thrushes on the 31st. A typically confiding Waxwing delighted many observers as it posed in one of the gardens at Whitehall Village.

The 31st was an excellent day back on the Reserve too, when we discovered a Little Bunting feeding in the flattened oats. It was seen almost daily, well into 1994 – the most northerly wintering record ever in Great Britain.

This large pipit found in late October may well have been a Blyth's

The Reserve drive in winter

1994

The wintering Little Bunting was seen almost daily during the cold spell at the beginning of 1994, by which time it became almost tame, allowing approach to within a few feet on occasions. It could be quite difficult to locate however, as the "tick" call was by now much more subdued, probably as a result of the bird being settled, although on occasions it would revert to a more strident version, usually when taking to the wing.

Reed Buntings and a party of 5 Corn Buntings were often seen feeding in the oats during this icy spell of weather, and every day or so we would rake over a small area of oat stalks to expose more seed. Rock Doves too often fed in the area – all truly wild birds, as Stronsay has a large number of breeding pairs. One rocky inlet close to the reserve is still known as 'Pigeon Geo'.

On the 12th April I spent most of the day sketching on the kitchen table and kept noticing how disturbed all the birds were around the Meikle Water, just over a mile away and directly in front of the house. It seemed that there was even more panic in the air than when any of the regular Peregrines flew over, and each time I noticed the disturbance I dashed outside and scanned the whole sky hoping to find the culprit. This happened on at least twenty occasions that day and I had given up all hope as I went out to help Sue, who had just passed the kitchen window on her way to light a bonfire.

As I stepped outside I almost bumped into her. She was looking up towards the loch and pointing, and there, drifting slowly towards us was a magnificent white Gyrfalcon.

We just stood transfixed as it drifted past the reserve less than 50yds from where we stood, and we watched it heading slowly off to the north and finally out of sight.

I should have known! There had been an eerie sinister feeling in the air that day, something I had only ever noticed once before – on Fair Isle in December 1992 when the culprit was again a beautiful white Gyrfalcon. Not only do they cause total panic among the larger birds, it seems that when one is in the vicinity all the small species disappear completely, giving the feeling of 'death' in the air.

We went back indoors elated hardly daring to hope to see it again, but over the next few days we saw it several times and were treated to some fantastic aerobatics as it hurtled towards the wintering duck flock on the Meikle Water. Twice it flew over the Reserve and on the 14th we discovered it feeding on a duck at the edge of the loch where two Hooded Crows were trying to steal its prey, lunging in from both sides alternately. After a few minutes

The Gyrfalcon treated us to some fantastic aerobatics

it tired of their attention and picking up the corpse flew off south. We saw it just once more, on the 18th, and sadly a group of keen birders who came up from the south of England a few days later hoping to see the bird were doomed to disappointment.

The reserve pond and 'false' ditch shortly after construction. Both are big attractions to migrants

During April we constructed the 'false' ditch which we connected to the large pond in the drive. It was lined with polythene to retain moisture and constructed in such a way that we could reconstitute the muddy bottom by allowing the pond to overflow into it. It worked so well and looked so natural that within a month of its construction a pair of Meadow Pipits had built a nest in the side of the ditch from which they raised four young. The ditch can be kept moist all through the summer and is a great attraction to many species.

Friday the 13th May was – as in 1988 – the best day for spring migrants. Two Bluethroats were found singing within twenty yards of each other and we were so enthralled with them, their throats absolutely gleaming in the bright sunshine, that we almost failed to notice a species we had never seen on Stronsay before –

a Tree Sparrow. Fortunately it was chirping away on a nearby fence-wire and eventually drew our attention to it.

Tree Sparrow – new for the island

The most encouraging aspect of 1994 was the number of calling Corncrakes on the island. At least four were heard and it is possible that at least two pairs bred successfully. A visiting couple's patience was rewarded in early June when one bird ran across the public road in front of their car as they waited in a lay-by.

Looking north from the Reserve towards Whitehall Village

At this time of year the sun barely dips below the horizon and Mill Bay is generally flat calm.

We have often speculated as to what is the 'best bush for birds' in Great Britain. On Stronsay we have our own contender, an elder bush tucked behind a row of deserted farm buildings. By 1993 we had found Greenish, Yellow-browed, Barred, Icterine and Marsh Warblers feeding among the branches as well as Red-backed

Shrike and Bluethroat, and autumn 1994 was destined to move it further up the rankings!

Autumn that year began rather later than usual but it certainly started with a bang! On the 24th there was a big 'fall', and among the birds seen early that day were 2 Wrynecks and 2 Barred Warblers.

On reaching our favourite elder bush at about 11am I could see the local House Sparrow flock preening and enjoying the sunshine in the upper branches and casually scanned through them. Sitting right out in the open on the top branch was our first Common Rosefinch for the bush – but far better was to follow!

I immediately returned to the house where we were expecting a guest who was due to arrive on the late-morning boat.

Knowing she would want to see at least some of the species we had discovered I asked her which she would prefer to go and look for. The Rosefinch was top of her list so we headed straight for the elder bush.

By the time we arrived the Rosefinch had disappeared but there, in the same bush, was the warbler we had wanted to see on the island more than any other – an Arctic. And there it was, long super-cilium, wing-bars, grey-washed underparts, dagger-like bill – the complete works!

Our island warbler list had been lop-sided until now, with 5 Greenish Warblers and no Arctics. This had redressed the balance somewhat, and how fortunate that find was! If it had not been for

There in our favourite bush was an Arctic Warbler!

the arrival of our visitor it is very unlikely that I would have returned to the elder bush that day, and by the following day the warbler had gone.

Using a piece of old farm machinery close to the bush as a 'hide' I was lucky enough to obtain a series of excellent photographs of the Arctic Warbler, again helping with its acceptance by the BBRC. This brought our island warbler list to 21 species.

The 25th August saw more migrants including a Wryneck and a Red-backed Shrike together, and by now the rather predictable reserve Common Rosefinch. It is quite possible that we now have the best site in Great Britain for seeing this species on autumn migration!

September 1st brought 2 Barred Warblers to the garden where they could be watched at very close range from the kitchen window as they clattered about among the branches of the small willow immediately outside.

Unfortunately not all the interesting birds are as obliging as Barred warblers and this was never illustrated more vividly than during a big 'fall' on the 30th. Strong SE winds had brought many birds to the island overnight but by dawn the wind had swung to the SW. This made finding them more difficult, as by now they tended to be in areas normally exposed to the wind during big influxes, and that morning we found ourselves searching 'in negative' – looking along what to us seemed the 'wrong' side of walls etc. Many of our normally productive sites were deserted.

The unpredictability of bird watching is one of its greatest attractions and in particular those times when one has set out in the hope of finding one particular species and discovered something even better!

On the 10th October I had set out with a friend hoping to find a Ruff to add to his holiday list and as we scanned a large flock of Golden Plover found a much rarer wader – Pectoral Sandpiper, and once again a new bird for the island.

A Richard's Pipit discovered at Lower Whitehall on 12th October was found within ten yards of the spot where we had found one on our first stay on the island in 1977.

SE winds and drizzle are well-known as just about the perfect combination for bringing migrants to Orkney and Shetland in particular, although they are hardly ideal conditions for those of us looking for them!

The 21st of October 1994 produced such conditions and we had to return to the house several times that day to dry out. It was without doubt one of the best days on record.

A bunting first seen in the road at Lower Whitehall proved to be Orkney's first Cirl Bunting although its elusive behaviour did cause us a problem at first.

Cirl Bunting – the first to be seen in Scotland since 1976

The most recent record for Scotland prior to our bird had been in 1976 when a ringed individual was caught on the Isle of May in June. Interestingly it had been ringed as a juvenile the previous July in Sussex.

Shortly after seeing the Cirl Bunting we discovered a Dusky Warbler, but this one was far less obliging than the bird of '93. Giving excellent initial views, it disappeared into an area of weeds and was never seen again.

There was almost immediate compensation however when we received a call from a nearby house where a visiting relative had discovered a Pallas's Warbler in the garden! It too proved rather elusive but eventually all those islanders and visitors who went to see this 'jewel' of a bird were rewarded with amazing views as it often hovered above the grass in the tiny garden there.

Only the second island record and far more obliging than the first which was seen in October 1990. This second bird was present for two days whilst the first was watched for just thirty seconds and then never seen again.

There was a large invasion of 'northern' Bullfinches around this time and parties could be seen all over the island. Much bulkier-looking than their southern counterparts all those seen were eating nettle-seeds, often clinging to the stems.

A second Dusky Warbler was found in the Manse garden on 28th October and this bird, unlike the individual of the 21st, gave excellent views as it fed among the hebe and fuchsia bushes. On alighting in vegetation etc. Dusky Warblers invariably flick their tails up – a very useful field-mark when given only brief initial views, and this second bird performed admirably, flicking its tail up as it dived into cover after each of the many short flights we witnessed. This action gives the species the appearance of a tiny short-tailed 'sylvia' warbler.

Pallas's Warbler – found in a nearby garden

The immaculate male Black-throated Thrush seen in late April 1995

1995

Much of the first three months of 1995 was taken up preparing the illustrations for this book and as a consequence we had very little time for birdwatching.

Spring migration had been slow, but at the end of April we were in for a real surprise. A beautiful full summer-plumaged male Black-throated Thrush had been found on one of the farms, feeding in a field of neaps, and we managed to see it that same evening – just in time, as that night saw the fatal combination of clear skies and a NW wind and the bird was never seen again.

The bird was a stunning combination of black, white and grey, and 'front-on' almost had the appearance of a Ring Ouzel 'in negative'. The call was a soft Blackbird-like 'chuckle' and in flight the intense black of the throat and upper-breast gave it a 'front-heavy' appearance.

This really was a 'just in time' sighting as two days later the neaps had been collected and the field ploughed.

A group of children from the Stronsay School visited the Reserve in late spring and helped sow one of the wild-flower mounds in the drive. Just as the group were preparing the ground for sowing, the first Arctic Skua of the year flew right overhead.

Three small areas of oats were sown at around the same time and the same wild-flower mix as that used on the mound was added to the oat-seed. Just a few days later the first of three spring Bluethroats was found singing in a ditch.

Finding a Rosefinch feeding on dandelions at the end of the garden in late May, we immediately alerted two of our guests over their mobile telephone. They finally arrived at the house 30 minutes later and showed us a video they had just taken.

Amazingly they had found a party of 3 Rosefinches together as they drove the short distance to the Reserve. But they were not so lucky a day or so later when a beautiful male Subalpine Warbler turned up a few hours after they had left the island!

Birdwatching can be like that!

The male Subalpine Warbler of late May 1995

Stop Press:
A pair of American Wigeon from 19th-22nd June 1995 bring the island species total up to 232 in less than eight years!

Finale

So it can be done! In 1988 we inherited what were probably the most uninteresting five acres of land on the island and yet within just a few years it has been transformed into one of the best-known sites in the U.K. for rare migrants. By careful planting and a mixture of good luck and skilled management an amazing number of species have been recorded on the reserve, and including those seen flying over the list now stands at 179 – just one short of the number of species we recorded from the Fair Isle shop during our time there. The oats in particular have been a great success and this is reflected in the fact that three species of rare bunting have been attracted to the area and Common Rosefinches are now almost a regular feature of the autumn.

The island itself is now well and truly on the ornithological map with 5 species new to Orkney since 1988 and two others 'pending' with the British Birds Rarities Committee.

What do the next few years have in store? Who knows or even wants to know? What is certain is that there will be more new birds, more surprises and no doubt disappointments, but it is the unpredictability of birdwatching that makes it so interesting. Just imagine what would be discovered if there were many such sites as our own, dotted around the coastline of Britain. If land prices were low enough throughout the country many of us could set up our own 'reserve'. The contribution to ornithology and conservation could be immense.

Radde's Warbler (bottom) and Dusky Warbler.
Two of the many species of rare warbler found by the author on Stronsay.
The first British record of Dusky Warbler was found on the off-shore island
of Auskerry (part of Stronsay) in 1913

Summer in the Reserve yard

BIRDS SEEN ON STRONSAY SINCE 1987

(The list order generally follows 'Voous 1977'
and the names generally follow 'British Birds' 1978)

* denotes birds seen from the Reserve

Red-throated Diver*	Greylag Goose*	Common Scoter*
Black-throated Diver*	Canada Goose*	Velvet Scoter
Great Northern Diver*	Snow Goose	Goldeneye*
Little Grebe	Barnacle Goose*	Red-breasted Merganser*
Red-necked Grebe*	Brent Goose*	Goosander*
Slavonian Grebe*	Ruddy Shelduck	Honey Buzzard*
Fulmar*	Shelduck*	Red Kite*
Sooty Shearwater	Mandarin	Marsh Harrier*
Manx Shearwater	Wigeon*	Hen Harrier*
Storm Petrel*	Gadwall	Sparrowhawk*
Leach's Petrel*	Teal*	Buzzard*
Gannet*	Mallard*	Kestrel*
Cormorant*	Pintail*	Merlin*
Shag*	Garganey*	Hobby
Grey Heron*	Shoveller*	Gyrfalcon*
Mute Swan*	Pochard*	Peregrine*
Whooper Swan*	Tufted Duck*	Quail*
Bean Goose*	Scaup	Pheasant*
Pink-footed Goose*	Eider*	Water Rail*
White-fronted Goose*	Long-tailed Duck*	Spotted Crake

Corncrake*
Moorhen*
Coot*
Oystercatcher*
Little Ringed Plover
Ringed Plover*
Dotterel
American Golden Plover
Golden Plover*
Grey Plover*
Lapwing*
Knot*
Sanderling*
Semi-palmated Sandpiper
Little Stint
Pectoral Sandpiper
Curlew Sandpiper
Purple Sandpiper*
Dunlin*
Ruff*
Jack Snipe*
Snipe*
Woodcock*
Black-tailed Godwit*
Bar-tailed Godwit*
Whimbrel*
Curlew*
Spotted Redshank*
Redshank*
Greenshank*
Green Sandpiper*
Wood Sandpiper*
Common Sandpiper*
Turnstone*
Red-necked Phalarope
Grey Phalarope
Pomarine Skua
Arctic Skua*

Long-tailed Skua*
Great Skua*
Little Gull*
Sabine's Gull
Black-headed Gull*
Common Gull*
Lesser Black-backed Gull*
Herring Gull*
Iceland Gull*
Glaucous Gull*
Great Black-backed Gull*
Kittiwake*
Sandwich Tern*
Common Tern*
Arctic Tern*
Roseate tern*
Little Tern*
Black Tern*
Guillemot*
Razorbill*
Black Guillemot*
Little Auk*
Puffin*
Rock Dove*
Woodpigeon*
Collared Dove*
Turtle Dove*
Cuckoo*
Snowy Owl
Long-eared Owl*
Short-eared Owl*
Nightjar
Swift*
Bee-eater*
Hoopoe
Wryneck*
Great Spotted Woodpecker*
Woodlark

Skylark*
Sand Martin*
Swallow*
House Martin*
Richard's Pipit*
Tawny Pipit
Olive-backed Pipit*
Tree Pipit*
Meadow Pipit*
Red-throated Pipit
Rock Pipit*
Yellow Wagtail*
Grey Wagtail
Pied Wagtail*
Waxwing
Wren*
Dunnock*
Robin*
Bluethroat
Black Redstart*
Redstart*
Whinchat*
Stonechat*
Wheatear*
Pied Wheatear
White's Thrush
Ring Ouzel*
Blackbird*
Black-throated Thrush
Fieldfare*
Song Thrush*
Redwing*
Mistle Thrush*
Grasshopper Warbler*
Sedge Warbler*
Marsh Warbler*
Reed Warbler*
Icterine Warbler

110

Subalpine Warbler	Pied Flycatcher*	Linnet*
Sardinian Warbler	Blue Tit	Twite*
Barred Warbler*	Tree-creeper	Redpoll*
Lesser Whitethroat*	Golden Oriole	Arctic Redpoll*
Whitethroat*	Red-backed Shrike*	Crossbill*
Garden Warbler*	Great Grey Shrike*	Common Rosefinch*
Blackcap*	Jackdaw*	Bullfinch*
Greenish Warbler	Rook*	Lapland Bunting*
Arctic Warbler	Carrion Crow*	Snow Bunting*
Pallas's Warbler	Raven*	Yellowhammer*
Yellow-browed Warbler*	Starling*	Cirl Bunting
Radde's Warbler	Rose-coloured Starling	Ortolan Bunting
Dusky Warbler	House Sparrow*	Rustic Bunting*
Wood Warbler*	Tree Sparrow	Little Bunting*
Chiffchaff*	Chaffinch*	Yellow-breasted Bunting*
Willow Warbler*	Brambling*	Reed Bunting*
Goldcrest*	Greenfinch*	Corn Bunting*
Spotted Flycatcher*	Goldfinch*	
Red-breasted Flycatcher	Siskin*	

Acknowledgements

A special thank-you to the people of Stronsay who all allow us access to their land and gardens. A thank-you too for all their kindness and enthusiasm, and the many telephone calls alerting us to birds. A big thank-you too to our many visitors, and in particular our regulars, who have contributed much to our ornithological records and to the success of the Reserve.

John and Sue Holloway
Stronsay Bird Reserve 1995

The oats and wild flowers on the Bird Reserve in September 1993.
The perfect combination for attracting seed-eating migrants

The Reserve is open all-year-round and has limited accommodation for a small number of guests. For details write, or Telephone: 01857 616363